SABLE ISLAND

D1453750

SABLE ISLAND

Tales of Tragedy and Survival
from the Graveyard of the Atlantic

HISTORY

by Johanna Bertin

To Bruce, my husband and best friend. Thank you.
And to those who love Sable Island
and seek to protect her from harm.

PUBLISHED BY ALTITUDE PUBLISHING CANADA LTD.
1500 Railway Avenue, Canmore, Alberta T1W 1P6
www.altitudepublishing.com
www.amazingstories.ca
1-800-957-6888

Extreme care has been taken to ensure that all information presented in
this book is accurate and up to date. Neither the author nor the
publisher can be held responsible for any errors.

Publisher	Stephen Hutchings
Series Editor	Diana Marshall
Editors	Jill Foran and Ros Penty
Digital Photo Colouring	Bryan Pezzi

We acknowledge the financial support of the Government
of Canada through the Book Publishing Industry Development
Program (BPIDP) for our publishing activities.

Altitude GreenTree Program
Altitude Publishing will plant twice as many trees as were used
in the manufacturing of this product.

National Library of Canada Cataloguing in Publication Data

Bertin, Johanna
Sable Island / Johanna Bertin.

(Amazing stories)
Includes bibliographical references.
ISBN 1-55439-010-9

1. Sable Island (N.S.)--History. I. Title.
II. Series: Amazing stories (Canmore, Alta.)

FC2345.S22B47 2006   971.6'99   C2006-900808-6

Amazing Stories® is a registered trademark of Altitude Publishing Canada Ltd.

Printed and bound in Canada by Friesens
2 4 6 8 9 7 5 3 1

Contents

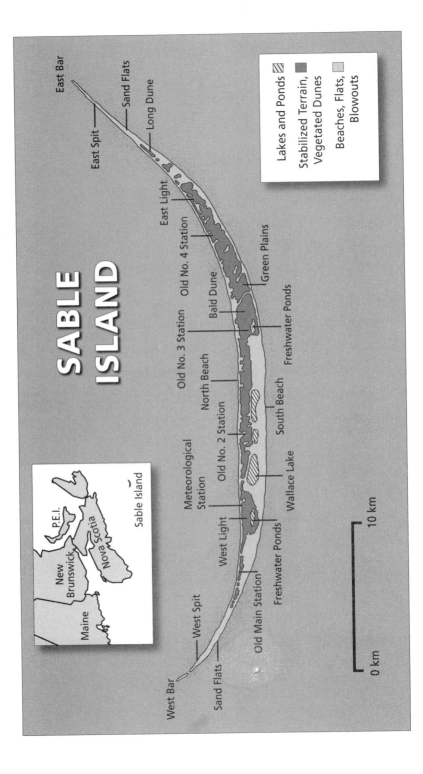

Prologue

In 1845, the American ship Eagle *struck the south shore of Sable Island, Nova Scotia, with such force that her hull drove deep into the sand, her mast broke, and her deckhouse shattered. She listed to port, beached like a whale at the waterline.*

The Eagle *carried 100 tons of bar copper from the Newfoundland mines at Twillingate. The weight of the cargo held the ship stationary, and over the next four years she mired deeper into the sand until only her timberheads were visible at low tide on a calm day. Then one winter, she disappeared entirely, entombed beneath the sand.*

In March 1860, the Eagle *appeared again. Thirteen-year-old James Farquahar, son of the keeper of the East End Station, had risen early, eager to see what the waves had driven onto the beach during the southeast gale of the evening before. James had lived on Sable Island for 11 years, and had heard the tales of ships that had gone down in the storms, of ships that had been driven up on the beach. But here was a ship resurfaced.*

Not only was the Eagle *visible, but the current and the waves had changed the sand bed and undermined the wreck, so that she had righted and then tipped onto her starboard side. The paint on her port side was fresh and did not look as if it had been submerged under sand and saltwater for 15 years.*

James peered into the ship's hold. The copper was still there, oxidized a dull green.

With the next storm, the Eagle *disappeared beneath the sand and water once again.*

Introduction
Why So Many Shipwrecks?

Sable Island lies about 160 kilometres east–southeast of Halifax, Nova Scotia, in one of the richest fishing grounds of the Atlantic Ocean and in the path of ships travelling the Great Circle Route between Europe and the Americas. More than 350 ships have wrecked on Sable's shores since 1583, earning it the name "Graveyard of the Atlantic."

From the air, the island appears a crescent, with its arms reaching up to the north. But Sable's arms disappear into the water at the elbow, and it is what lies under the surface that has so often brought ships to their demise. Sand bars and sand spits extend for 74 kilometres under the water beyond the west tip of the island, and for 52 kilometres at the eastern end. This island, which measures 48 kilometres in length on the surface, is, in reality, more than 160 kilometres from end to end.

Sable Island

Sable Island is not a static landmass, but rather a shape-shifting sand beach. Major storms change its contours, shortening one end of the island and lengthening the other so that, at times, it appears to move west or east. Dunes reach up to 26 metres in height, but much of the island is at such a low elevation, and more than a kilometre in width, that a ship's captain approaching the south shore on a calm day would be able to see the ocean waves lapping onto the north shore. On a stormy day, he would run aground before he saw Sable.

There are no rocks on the island, and only one tree, and the grey sand presents little contrast to the ocean colour, except where the marram grass shivers in the wind, or the freshwater ponds shimmer in the sunlight.

And then there's the fog that shrouds Sable Island 125 days a year, and the storms, hurricanes, and August Gales that track up the Atlantic coast and hammer the island. The warm Gulf Stream travels east off its south beach, and the cold Labrador Current travels west along its north beach; in conflict with each other, they create a vortex, a whirlpool around the island that has sucked many ships into its whorl.

It is no surprise that so many ships have foundered at Sable Island. It is more a wonder that any survived the foundering.

Chapter 1
The Courtier: Sir Humphrey Gilbert

I n the spring of 1583, Sir Humphrey Gilbert prepared to set sail for the New World. He was an ambitious man, a soldier and a sailor, a man of education and court connections through his half-brother, Sir Walter Raleigh, the rumoured lover of Queen Elizabeth I of England.

That same queen had ordered Gilbert to assert England's claim over Newfoundland and of the land "200 leagues to the North and the South," and most importantly over her fisheries. England depended on Newfoundland cod now that she was barred from fishing off Iceland. Gilbert was also to collect ore samples, so that England could determine possible mineral riches.

Gilbert's assignment pleased him, for it offered him the possibility of much wealth and prestige. He planned to found colonies in Cape Breton, Nova Scotia, and down the eastern seaboard of the Americas. It was this dream, and a chance meeting with a Portuguese sailor, that would take Gilbert to Sable Island.

On June 15, 1583, Gilbert sailed from Plymouth with a fleet of five vessels: the *Delight*, the *Raleigh*, the *Golden Hind*, the *Swallow*, and the *Squirrel*. The excitement he felt was tempered by the almost immediate return to port of the *Raleigh*, her crew decimated by a contagious illness. Gilbert continued on, his force diminished by one, but a very significant one, for the *Raleigh* had carried a good part of the provisions.

For weeks they sailed west across the Atlantic. Storms blew them off course, delayed their passage, and used up their provisions. Men died and were dropped overboard. When the crew of the *Swallow* sighted an eastbound ship, they boarded her, stole her provisions and sails, and took the crew's clothing to replace their own worn garments. Gilbert's men, sailors in the British navy, were little more than pirates.

On August 3, 1583, Gilbert finally reached Newfoundland. He summoned, then threatened the captains of the fishing fleets. He would have their allegiance or he would have their ships. His dominance established, he set out to gather ore samples. He had fewer men to do his bidding, for Gilbert's arrogance and abusive outbursts had caused many of his crew to desert and take to the woods.

One of his men came to him with the story of a Portuguese sailor who told of an island in the North Atlantic where cattle roamed. The information seemed reliable, for the man said he had been there himself, 30 years earlier, when his countrymen had unloaded the animals from their ships. Gilbert, reeling from his experience crossing the Atlantic, immediately saw the potential of an island stocked with provisions for ships. Such a find would be a coup for this courtier-turned-explorer. The island could be established as a veritable storehouse for British sailors. Its location was strategic, lying off the shore of North America, yet in the very centre of the shipping routes to the New World and the West Indies. Cattle and hogs could be left to roam free, ready food for sailors of the British fleet. (Gilbert seems not to have questioned why a Portuguese sailor, a man whose country was an enemy of England, would not only tell him about Sable Island, but would also suggest that an Englishman stock his ships with Portuguese-owned cattle.)

Gilbert had maps and documents aboard the *Delight*. They supported the man's tale and mentioned "the Isle de Sablon (Island of Sand), which is very full of cattell and swine." One of the documents, "Instructions for a Voyage of Reconnaissance to North America," included one very significant detail: it cautioned mariners to approach the island in daylight only.

On August 20, 1583, Gilbert left Cape Race, Newfoundland, with the *Delight*, the *Golden Hind*, and Gilbert's own *Squirrel*. He had sent the *Swallow* back to England with those of his men who were ill and unfit to carry out further exploration.

For six days the remaining men sailed without sighting land. Then the fog rolled in. No longer were the sextants any use in navigation, for they worked by taking a sighting from the sun or stars. The navigators now depended on "dead reckoning," using a ship's speed and direction to estimate her position. The ships were isolated from each other, invisible in the blanket of suffocating fog that soaked them as if they'd been in a rainstorm.

On the seventh day, August 27, 1583, the fog lifted and the ships' captains and navigators conferred on the best course. Richard Clarke, navigator on the *Delight*, suggested a course of west–southwest.

Gilbert, no navigator, but a man accustomed to issuing orders, responded with a command to head west–north-west. William Cox, navigator on the *Golden Hind*, sided with Clarke. In vain they reasoned with Gilbert, but he insisted that Clarke's reckoning was wrong. Clarke and Cox were adamant. Gilbert threatened that they either follow his command or never show themselves in England again.

The fleet headed west–northwest and, despite the disagreement, the crew of the *Delight* seemed in fair spirits, for the sound of trumpets, drums, and fifes was heard by the men on the following ships. Later, they said that it had sounded like the "Swanne that singeth before her death."

During the night, the wind rose to gale force and shifted to the southeast. The rain came — heavy, driving rain that diminished what little visibility they had. Gilbert's ships had met the August Gales, storms of such ferocity that they tore sails from masts and snapped masts in two.

Cox, on the *Golden Hind*, sighted land and signalled to

the *Delight*, but what he took, in the pre-dawn light, to be white cliffs were in fact enormous white breakers, rolling and tumbling over the sand bars that front Sable Island. Driven by the wind, and carried by the power of the waves, the *Delight* gathered momentum and struck a sand bar with such force that her keel cut into it and was held fast by the sand.

Waves like green glass mountains swept over the ship, snapping her masts and sweeping them — along with the crew and the rigging — into the roiling water. The ship's seams split apart, and the ore samples from Newfoundland, together with Gilbert's books, maps, and charts, bled into the sand of Sable Island. The *Delight* caved in on herself and disappeared beneath the waves, as if sucked into the sand.

The *Golden Hind* and the *Squirrel* managed to turn before they, too, were swept onto the bars. They returned when the weather calmed, but found no survivors from the *Delight*. On August 31, Gilbert headed home, his fleet reduced to two ships, his crew demoralized and on the verge of mutiny. He had founded no colonies and had lost the all-important ore samples, the flagship *Delight*, and 100 crew-members. Now, short of provisions and poorly clothed, he and his men began the long sea voyage back to England.

Gilbert may have been a more experienced man, but he was no wiser. He ignored warnings that the *Squirrel* was over-gunned and at risk of foundering in heavy seas, and he died with his men when she sank in a storm north of the Azores.

Edward Haies and the *Golden Hind* arrived in Falmouth on September 22, 1583. His report on the disastrous mission, especially the destruction of the *Delight* and the loss of all aboard, gave birth to the conviction that Sable Island had "a bad repute for ship wrecks."

But Haies's recounting was wrong in one very important detail.

Chapter 2
The Pirate:
Richard Clarke

E dward Haies had underestimated the survival skills of navigator Richard Clarke. Clarke called himself a privateer, claiming to have a commission from Queen Elizabeth I authorizing him to attack and pillage Portuguese shipping. But he'd never been awarded such papers, and was in reality a pirate. Before joining Gilbert's expedition, he had been master of his own ship and had sailed the waters around Newfoundland and the Grand Banks. He knew the area intimately; he could read the seas and the sky, and smell a storm upon the air. And he garnered far more respect than Gilbert did.

Clarke did not depend entirely on his ship's provisions for food. The day before the *Delight* struck Sable Island, one of his men had shot a black duck. The crew, eager for fresh meat, had lowered a pinnace (a small boat holding 12) so they could retrieve the game. When they had returned to the ship, they tied the pinnace to one of the lines, rather than hoisting it on board again. All night long the pinnace had trailed in the wake of the flagship.

When the *Delight* struck the sand bar, the force of the impact threw crewmembers into the water. Two of the crew, stronger than the others, swam to the pinnace and heaved themselves in. Then they rescued others, one of whom was Clarke — a stroke of luck or design, for they needed a navigator above all else if they were to survive.

They continued to pick up survivors, but there were few. Only 14 of the 100 men on the *Delight* made it into the pinnace. Some, like Clarke, had injuries. All were wet and exhausted. They had no supplies, no food, and no extra clothing. Most significantly, they had only one oar.

They called to Captain Maurice Browne, but he refused to abandon the *Delight* and urged them to try to make it to the island. Clarke could do little but let the pinnace take them where the currents directed, using the oar as a rudder to keep the boat pointed into the waves. He later wrote that it "looked every moment of an houre when the Sea would eat them up, the boate being so little and so many men in her, and so foule weather." Miraculously, they were not caught in the vortex around Sable Island. If they had been, they might have journeyed day after day, only to find themselves in the very same place.

By the third night, they were in acute pain from starvation and considered sacrificing some so that the others might survive. It was not so much a question of food, for they had none, but the boat was overladen and in danger of swamping. Edward Headly, a soldier, suggested they cast lots and those who lost be thrown overboard. He offered himself as the first sacrifice. Clarke would be exempt from the lottery because he was an officer. More important, as navigator, he was their only hope of making landfall.

Clarke rejected Headly's offer and insisted they would live or die together. The overcrowding did have one advantage: the men benefited from the body heat that they shared in such close quarters. Clarke, perhaps to hearten them, told them he knew where they were and that he hoped to reach land in three or four days.

But three days later, the group still hadn't seen land. Headly and another man had died and been slid overboard, after the survivors took what clothing they could off of them. The rest were suffering greatly from hypothermia, injuries that they had incurred in the wreck, and starvation. In their five days at sea, they had only "the weedes that swamme in the Sea, and salt water to drink." Clarke advised them to drink their own urine instead.

The foul weather continued. The men saw the sun only once in their long trip, and at night the clouds blocked out the stars. On the sixth day, they gave up. They were in agony from the cramps of starvation, and from the pain of the boils on their bodies caused by salt irritation and wet clothing. But that night, the fog lifted, and Clarke could finally see the stars. He promised the men they would reach land on the seventh day. The men had no hope left, but neither did they have the strength to do anything but remain in the boat and take turns manning the oar, keeping the pinnace on the course that Clarke directed, borne along by a southerly wind and the Gulf Stream current.

The morning dawned on the seventh day and, true to Clarke's word, the survivors made landfall. Astonishingly, the pinnace had journeyed from Sable Island to Newfoundland's south coast in the same time it had taken Gilbert's fleet to sail the opposite journey.

The men crawled onto the shore, the strongest finding food for the weakest. They lived off the land, slowly making their way westward until they met the crew of a French Basque whaler preparing to sail home from a whaling expedition in the Gulf of St. Lawrence. They asked for and were granted passage to France.

It was December 1583 before Clarke arrived back in England, nearly four months after Edward Haies had reported his death. The story of his shipwreck and journey added to the mystique of Sable Island. But soon, there would be a story of survival on the island that would eclipse even Clarke's.

Chapter 3
The Settler:
Marquis de la Roche

ith time, the story of Richard Clarke and his amazing journey made its way to the French court of Henry IV. There it came to the attention of an aristocrat by the name of Troilus de Mesgouez, Marquis de la Roche.

La Roche was 13 years old when he became a page at the court of Henry III. When he was 25, Catherine de Medici awarded him the governorship of Brittany. In 1578, Henry III bestowed further honours on him and gave him lieutenant generalship of a vast territory that included most of eastern Canada ("of Hochelaga, of the newfound lands, of La Bras d'Or, of the River of the Great Bay of Norumbega and the Isles de Sable and grounds adjacent of the aforesaid provinces and rivers.") In essence, Clarke had been shipwrecked on La Roche's property.

La Roche had not yet had an opportunity to claim

his territory. The French Wars of Religion had erupted, and La Roche, who fought on the side of the Huguenots, was captured, deprived of his estates, and imprisoned in the dungeons of Nantes. When Henry IV came to the throne, he restored La Roche's fortune. More important to La Roche, he renewed his letters patent in 1598.

La Roche was now 60 years old, but eager to take advantage of the title that gave him free reign to profit from the fisheries and fur trade of the New World. He recognized the key strategic location of *Isle de Sables* and decided to make it his base of operation. What he needed were settlers for his planned military and trading outpost. Lacking volunteers, he went to the Parlement de Rouen and petitioned for 50 of the sturdiest convicts and beggars. They would provide the workforce. Ten soldiers were conscripted to keep order and man the military outpost.

In 1598, they set out from France in two ships. La Roche commanded the *Catherine*, and Thomas Chefdostel de Voteuille, his navigator, commanded the *Françoise*. They sailed directly to Sable Island and, unlike Gilbert, had no difficulty making anchor and rowing to shore.

La Roche was astounded at the beauty of the island. From their anchor at the north beach, he gazed at sand dunes that measured 26 metres in height, with steep slip faces. Yet, farther along the beach, the dunes were so low that he could see the ocean on the other side of the island. The scent of sweet grass and salt mingled with that of wild orchids and strawberries. It seemed like a heavenly place for his planned settlement.

The Settler: Marquis de la Roche

The dunes along the north and south shores of Sable Island change shape with each storm, sometimes exposing artifacts from shelters of old.

The conscripts quickly unloaded the provisions and set about building a settlement on the north shore, by the narrow opening to the freshwater lake (later named Lake Wallace). In quick succession, they built a fort with a storehouse, living quarters, and a magazine. Shipwrecks provided them with all the lumber and copper nails they needed.

La Roche placed Commander Querbonyer of the militia in charge of the conscripted settlers, with orders to seize any ships that fished or traded in furs without authorization. The men were to trap on behalf of La Roche, but they were not to enter into trade themselves. Then La Roche and Chefdostel set sail for Newfoundland, intending to claim fur and fishing rights for France.

In September, La Roche headed back to Sable, but,

plagued by storms, he missed the island entirely and returned to France. He did not worry unduly about his settlers, for Sable Island was less rugged and warmer than the mainland, and it had an abundance of fresh water. There was also plenty of food — the "cattel and swine" left by the Portuguese in the 1540s could be supplemented with fish, duck, sea birds, and seals. La Roche had explored the island and had seen evidence of wild cranberries and blueberries. No doubt the settlers would also obtain additional provisions from the ships that they seized.

La Roche never returned to Sable Island, but every year he sent supplies through Chefdostel. Then, in 1602, La Roche was again thrown into jail, this time by a rival at court, and deliveries to Sable Island ceased.

On Sable Island, conditions deteriorated. The men no longer tended the gardens, but instead relied on hunting and fishing. When their clothing rotted from age and wear, they fashioned other garments from the skins of cattle and seal. More important, the balance of power had shifted, and the soldiers were no longer in charge. First, the ex-convicts murdered Commander Querbonyer, then Captain Cassez, master of the magazine. Chaos reigned.

In 1603, Henry IV sent Chefdostel back to Sable Island to determine whether the island could support a permanent colony. Chefdostel found only 11 of the original 60 men still alive. Forty-eight had been murdered — the 10 soldiers and 38 of the 50 settlers. Chefdostel's crew rounded up the survivors and took them back to France after confiscating the furs that they'd harvested in their five years on the island.

But one person would not leave. The Franciscan monk who had been charged with the spiritual care of the settlers, and had served on the island all this time, declared himself too ill to face the long sea voyage. He preferred to die in his hut and let "the winds and the sands ... charge themselves with my burial."

Upon returning to France, Chefdostel presented the convict settlers, garbed as they had been at Sable Island, at the court of Henry IV. One of the courtiers remarked that they resembled the "river Gods of old," so long and matted was their hair and beard and so curiously were they dressed in their sealskins. Henry IV found them piteous and, rather than hanging them for the murders of 48 people (as La Roche requested), pardoned them and gave them 50 ecus each. He also awarded them the value of the pelts they had harvested. It was La Roche who died in poverty.

While La Roche's settlement could not be deemed a success, it was the earliest official European settlement in Canada. Henry IV never re-established a settlement on Sable Island, but the convicts did prove that the island could be inhabited year round, and that it held a wealth of seal and walrus. That richness led to yet another of the many efforts to plunder the island.

Chapter 4
The Sealer: John Rose

In 1633, the ship *Mary and Jane* ran aground at Sable Island. Her captain, John Rose of Boston, expected to find only a desolate sand spit. Instead, he marvelled at the sight of "800 cattle, small and great, all red, and the largest he ever saw." The cattle, descendents of those left by the Portuguese, were not the only surprise. Rose and his men had stepped onto the breeding ground of the harp and hooded seal. Sable Island was a virtual heaven for a sealer like John Rose.

The *Mary and Jane* was beyond repair, so Rose and his crew built a yawl from the wreckage of the larger ship. In the months that it took, they fished for sole and plaice in the freshwater lake close to the northwest beach, hunted the black fox and seal for their pelts, and studied the sea-morse (walrus). Finally, they completed the yawl and set sail for the mainland, arriving at La Hève colony, Acadia, and its Fort Sainte Marie-de-Grace near present-day Lunenburg. There, Rose and his men received shelter from Isaac Razilly, governor of Acadia, and his brother, Claude. Naturally, Rose shared the story of his four-month adventure on Sable Island, and told them of the hundreds of cattle roaming free. What Rose didn't know was that only weeks before his arrival, the Company of New France had given Sable Island to the Razillys for their "personal domain." The Razillys were keen to benefit from this new and unexpected bounty. Rose had hoped to make his way back to Boston. Instead, the Razillys bullied him into leading an expedition back to Sable Island.

Once there, the Acadians constructed shelters from the lumber of ships that had foundered on Sable Island. Then, over several months, they slaughtered 560 cattle, not for their meat, but for their hides. They left the carcasses to rot on the dunes.

When Razilly's men had decimated the herd, they returned to La Hève. Rose at last made his way back to Boston, where he formed the Boston Merchant Expedition with two others to hunt seal and morse on Sable Island. In June 1635, his partners, Mr. Graves in the *James* and Mr. Hodges in the *Rebecka*, set out for Sable Island. They took with them a house, a shallop, two mastiffs, and 12 seal hunters and would leave them there for two years. But first, they built storerooms big enough to hold two years' worth of hunting.

In mid-January, the hunters prepared for the arrival of the seals that came to the island's northeast bar to whelp.

When the pups were 25 days old, the men crept up on the herd, positioning themselves between the pups and the sea. Each man carried a six-foot-long (1.8 m) club made of oak or ash. One end had a piece of steel with a spike on one side and a blade on the other. The hunter would pick his prey, bludgeon the seal, and then insert the blade into the wound, removing the pelt with a few cuts.

Sometimes the seals would attack the men, but they had little defence against the clubs. The men took the pelts and peeled the fat off the carcasses to render it down for oil to use in their lamps — even though it smelled dreadful and smoked terribly, blacking the walls of their home. They took the seals' livers and ate them as a delicacy. Then, like the French before them, they left the carcasses to rot on the sand. Sharks swam close, attracted by the smell of blood, and the men stayed high out of the water. When the seal harvest was over, Rose's men next massacred the walruses for their ivory tusks.

In August 1637, the company sent 20 hunters to Sable Island to relieve the previous crew. But the hunters weren't able to find the island in the fog and returned to Boston. In September, they set out again; this time, they made land and replaced the men. Amazingly, the departing hunters claimed they had not had one case of illness in the two years.

By March 1639, when the company was scheduled to collect them, the sealers had a bounty of skins and ivory. But the ship that had been sent wrecked on the beach, and her crew, like so many before and after, was forced to build a small boat from the wreck of the larger ship. Unable to carry much more than themselves and some of the hunters, the men of the Boston Merchant Expedition left the pelts, ivory, and oil behind, hidden in the dunes and guarded by the mastiffs and a few men.

It would be another two years before the merchants of Boston could replace their ship and mount another expedition to Sable Island. This time, they brought back the hunters and part of the bounty from the previous expedition. And they again left fresh hunters behind to continue the harvest.

On August 8, 1641, Rose, by now a very rich man, sent one last ship to bring back 400 pairs of seamorse teeth (worth 300 pounds sterling), 12 tons of seal oil, and countless seal and fox pelts. The Boston Merchant Expedition had made 1500 pounds sterling from their Sable Island enterprise, but they had all but extinguished the walrus.

It would be treasure hunters of a different sort who would next visit Sable Island. They sought not its natural bounty, but ownership of the island.

Chapter 5
The Entrepreneur: André Le Mercier

ndré Le Mercier, pastor of the French Protestant church in Boston, Massachusetts, read his paper with interest. Sable Island was in the news again, the site of yet another shipwreck. But this particular wrecked ship was of more interest to Le Mercier than the others, for it wasn't a fishing boat or sealer. The latest vessel to meet her demise on Sable Island, on July 17, 1737, was a passenger ship called the *Cathrine*. There had been 202 persons on board — men, women, and children bound from Ireland to a new life in Boston. One hundred and two passengers had died in the wreck.

Le Mercier spent a moment thinking of the dead, and then he smiled. Here was the ammunition he needed. Since 1729, he had been seeking support for a French Huguenot settlement in Nova Scotia. He had petitioned Nova Scotia governor Richard Philipps to provide transport and start-up cash for 100 Huguenot refugees. Le Mercier, for his efforts, sought 5000 acres of arable farmland in which to develop his community.

His proposal had been rejected. Now, in the tragedy of the *Cathrine*, Le Mercier recognized an opportunity to once more petition the governor. His new proposal would be one that no one could refuse.

Le Mercier was aware of the dramatic impact of the loss of lives aboard the *Cathrine*. Both Canada and her neighbour to the south were seeking immigrants, and the vivid description of the pitiful cries of the castaways would deter those seeking travel to the Americas.

On April 1, 1738, Le Mercier and his associates proposed that they should settle the 10,000 acres of Sable Island and provide assistance to the shipwrecked. He had already transported cattle, swine, and sheep to the island and had built a house there — all at his own expense — in anticipation of his latest petition. All he asked for in return was that the current governor, Charles Armstrong, and the Nova Scotia Council forbid any persons from disturbing the settlement or its livestock.

Le Mercier was awarded "de jure" control of the island, and Governor Armstrong issued a proclamation forbidding any from "harming, molesting, or in any way interfering with Le Mercier and his associates in settling and stocking the island," in conducting a fishery, or in harvesting the seals for their oil and skins. But Le Mercier was not given ownership and refused to pay the penny an acre quit rent demanded by Her Majesty.

Armstrong knew he needed to support the shipwrecked, but he balked at giving the land away. Sable Island, as dangerous as it was, was strategically located in the east–west shipping lanes and could become only more valuable as a piece of real estate.

Le Mercier, proclamation notwithstanding, was having difficulty enforcing his rights. He wrote to Armstrong that, "evil-disposed fishermen keep stealing the cattle and goods." Le Mercier joined forces with John Gorham, commander of the Gorham Rangers. This was a strategic move, for Gorham and his Rangers had withstood the French siege of Annapolis Royal, and the Nova Scotia government was deeply in their debt. The pair sweetened their proposal by offering to build a lighthouse at Sable Island.

By this time, the Nova Scotia governor had again changed, and it was Governor Paul Mascarene who forwarded the petition to London and the Privy Council, along with a notation that Le Mercier still refused to pay the penny an acre requested. Le Mercier was adamant on this point. "As the land is low, boggy and sandy soil, with large ponds or settings of water occasioned by the overflowing of the tides," he thought a penny an acre too much for "what cannot be improved."

While Le Mercier and Gorham awaited the response of the Privy Council, they continued harvesting seals and fish and recorded the number of people they had saved from shipwrecks. They lived well, hunting black duck, fishing flounder and eels from the lake, and roasting clams from the beach. In late spring, gulls, ducks, and terns laid eggs in such quantity that Le Mercier's men collected them by the bucket load. They were having success growing turnips and other root crops, and harvested the wild blueberries, strawberries, and cranberries that grew in such profusion.

But such plenty enticed thieves, and in 1744, Le Mercier, in frustration, published a notice in the Boston papers: "They have sundry Times Stole our Cattle and our Goods, regarding neither the laws of God or of Man, neither Justice to me, or Humanity to shipwrec'd Men."

Le Mercier suspected fishermen of anchoring offshore and of coming onto the island at night to steal the livestock. He offered a 40-pound sterling reward for the identity of the perpetrators, as well as amnesty to any informer. But no one came forward, and he still hadn't heard from the Privy Council.

Then Le Mercier had a bit of luck. The next vessel to wreck on Sable's shores was the French corvette *Legere*, a ship in the Duc d'Anville's armada, which was bent on regaining Fort Louisburg from the British. Le Mercier's settlement hosted Captain Charles-Francois Guillimin and 17 of his crew for nine months, until British schooners arrived in June 1747 to take the men to prison in Boston. Surely now that Le Mercier had proved the value of Sable Island during a time of war, he would get his deed to the island. But no word came.

Gorham petitioned the French court, requesting reimbursement of the cost of caring for the shipwrecked French navy crew. But none came. For four more years, he and Le Mercier waited for payment from France, or land title from England. Finally, in 1751, Gorham travelled to England with the intention of presenting his petition in person. Instead, he died of smallpox.

By 1753, Le Mercier had had enough of waiting. Denied ownership of Sable Island, he nevertheless listed the island for sale. Forgotten were his concerns about low boggy land. Instead, he advertised a pasture in the middle of the ocean. He had no takers, and Le Mercier removed his staff and his livestock. By 1756, no domestic animals were left on Sable Island.

But soon, the number of animals on the island would increase again. Le Mercier may have given up his interest in the island, and Gorham may have passed away, but a third partner, Thomas Hancock, had his own plan for Sable Island.

Like Le Mercier and Gorham, Hancock was a Boston merchant, but he had military connections that earned him a great deal of money. The expulsion of the Acadians in 1755 brought him additional business opportunities. All Acadians who refused to declare their allegiance to the British Crown were to be expelled from their Nova Scotia land holdings. Not only did Hancock transport troops from New England to Nova Scotia, but his ships were leased to transport the Acadians to their new homelands. Hancock also benefitted from the confiscation of the Acadians' livestock. More than 18,000 cattle, 27,000 sheep, 13,000 swine, and 1600 horses were suddenly available for the taking. The horses were what interested Hancock.

Some he sold to settlers, some were shipped to plantations in the West Indies, and 60 of them were sent to Sable Island, transported there by a two-masted schooner from Grand Pré. Hancock never explained why he placed the 60 horses on the island, never even admitted to owning these animals seized from the Acadians, but family diaries recorded the event.

The crew that transported the horses was familiar with the dangers of Sable Island and approached the north shore at high tide — the one time of day when they could anchor in the open channel to Lake Wallace. They put the horses one by one in a sling attached to the gaff and boom and swung the sling out over the water. When the sling was released, the horse would drop into the lake. The healthy and strong ones swam to shore. Those that were debilitated by their roundup and the long journey along the west coast of Nova Scotia simply sank under the water and drowned.

Like so many others stranded on Sable Island before them, whether the horses lived or died would be determined by their strength and circumstances beyond their control. But soon, there would be an organized effort to help those who found themselves swept onto this island in the Atlantic.

Chapter 6
The Governor:
Sir John Wentworth

Nova Scotia governor Sir John Wentworth needed a presence on Sable Island. In 1797, he hired Andrew and William Miller as "keepers" who would live on the island and assist the shipwrecked. Wentworth was concerned about thieves, but he also suspected that ship owners were using Sable Island to defraud insurance companies. Four to five ships sank each year, with property loss amounting to hundreds of thousands of pounds sterling.

It was a lonely and harsh existence for the two keepers, and they left before their term was up. Wentworth recognized that a permanent settlement at Sable Island was long overdue. His motives were not purely humane — any money earned from salvage operations would make its way into the Nova Scotia government coffers. But one wreck in particular, that of the *Frances* in December 1799, forced the government to take action.

The *Frances* was a 208-ton government transport ship. The destruction of the ship was a major financial blow, but it was the loss of her cargo and personnel that caused widespread dismay and public outcry, for the *Frances* was carrying the personal property of Prince Edward, Duke of Kent. This fourth son of King George III was at that time stationed in Halifax as commander in chief of military forces in British North America. Eager to have the use of his personal belongings, he had arranged for his furniture, carriage and carriage horses, books, silver, and other household items to be brought over from England. The cargo was worth about 11,000 pounds sterling, but more important to the duke was the fact that Dr. Copeland, his personal physician and the man he'd entrusted with the responsibility of overseeing the shipment, had been aboard the ship, along with his wife and two children.

It had seemed to be a straightforward tragedy, but then the loss of the ship took on a criminal aspect. Uniforms of the 7th Fusiliers, the duke's regiment, appeared on the streets of Halifax, along with soldiers' caps. They could have only come from the wreck of the *Frances*. Wentworth decided it was time to determine just what was happening on Sable Island.

Knowing that the naval vessel *Trepassey* would soon be on her way to Newfoundland, Wentworth directed her commander, Lieutenant Joseph Scrambler, to lay over at Sable Island and search for survivors. Scrambler carried livestock for the use of future shipwreck victims, but his primary function was to look for signs of "wreckers," people who salvaged goods from shipwrecks, but who were also often suspected of luring ships to the shore with lanterns.

The *Trepassey* reached Sable Island on May 13, 1800. Lieutenant Scrambler found no one, alive or dead, but he did see a schooner anchored at the northeast spit. He tried to approach her, but the current prevented him from getting within hailing distance. At 4 p.m., he saw the schooner under sail and set a course that transected her path. Scrambler could now read her name: the *Dolphin*, a fishing schooner from Barrington, Nova Scotia. He suspected that she had a cargo of fish, sealskins, and sea oil. But he was also looking for other items, and he soon found them.

On board were several water- and salt-damaged trunks. One was clearly marked "HRH Prince Edward, No. 2." Another belonged to Captain Stirling of the 7th Regiment Foot Soldiers. Both were empty, but a third trunk contained two greatcoats, the livery worn by the duke's servants. Scrambler asked the commander of the *Dolphin*, Captain Reynolds, where he had acquired the greatcoats.

Reynolds claimed that two of his sealers, Coleman Crowell and Ziba Hunt, had overwintered on the island and had seen the vessel close to the northeast bar but had been unable to help because of the storm. These trunks were the only items salvaged from the ship. Scrambler saw no reason to doubt Reynolds's story, for he had heard tales of entire ships disappearing in storms around Sable Island.

Scrambler wrote his report, and then had his pilot deliver it and the retrieved items to Governor Wentworth. The pilot added his own news, for he had spoken directly with the sealers. His input supported Scrambler's report, but included some additional information that would change the face of Sable Island forever.

The sealers had told him that they had seen the *Frances* the day before the gale. The weather had been surprisingly good for the time of year, with just a light breeze — but the light wind had spelled trouble for the two-masted square-rigged transport ship. All day long she had tried to move away from the bar, but had made no progress. Then the weather changed and a tremendous gale struck from the southeast.

The sealers had taken shelter in their hut. In the morning, there had been no sign of the ship — she had disintegrated under the onslaught of the waves. The sealers said Captain Reynolds had lied about there being no cargo, for they had seen it wash up on shore later that day, along with the drowned carcasses of 12 shod horses, 2 sheep, 2 cows, and 1 bull. There had been barrels of biscuits, several cases of liquor, and parts of a small pinnace.

Wentworth was deeply concerned. Any salvage from shipwrecks was to be turned into the government, but he had long suspected that this law was being ignored. The pilot explained that there had been no survivors from the *Frances*, but there had been several corpses. One corpse had been that of a woman with a ring on her finger, the sealers had told him. Not being able to get the ring off, they had buried it with her.

The governor found this last bit of news disturbing. The Copelands had been well respected in Halifax, and he was too much the military man to believe that poor sealers would leave a ring on the finger of a dead woman. They were accustomed to butchering animals. Would they not just cut off her finger to get an obviously valuable ring? He ordered Captain Reynolds to report to Halifax for questioning about his seizure of salvage. Reynolds was charged, but escaped conviction because the court was unable to locate the two sealers — the prosecution's key witnesses.

To offset future losses, Wentworth hired Seth Coleman in June 1801 to study the potential for a full-time lifesaving station on the island. Coleman's first task, however, was to remove "A Man and a Woman of Wicked Character" who had landed on Sable "for the infamous, inhumane purpose of plundering, robbing, and causing shipwrecks."

Coleman found the squatters who, despite their reputation, seemed to be gainfully employed. The captain of a wrecked vessel had left Patrick and Mrs. King, their three children, and a cabin boy there to collect and dry a cargo of cotton that had washed ashore. Coleman left them to their task to go in search of a location for a lighthouse. He chose the eastern tip of the island, a spot that would be visible to those ships approaching North America from Europe. He completed his reconnaissance and then reported back that Sable Island could support both people and livestock.

First, Governor Wentworth sought support from the Nova Scotia legislature to discourage trespassers. In 1800, they passed an Act of Assembly that "prohibited residence on the island without a license." The penalty was up to six years in prison. Wentworth was given the authority to "appoint a person ... who should have the power to remove from it any Marauding Offender together with all goods found in his possession."

That same year, John Howe, publisher of the *Halifax Journal*, wrote a report full of lurid tales of wreckers, lost ships, and stolen property on Sable Island. Wentworth used it to support his request for the establishment of a lifesaving station. Then, two more ships wrecked at Sable Island — the *Packet* from Boston and the schooner *Industry* from Nova Scotia. As usual, there were no survivors. Wentworth knew that Nova Scotia needed to show the world that she was managing her sea lanes. Armed with Howe's report and the ever-increasing list of shipwrecks, he convinced the burghers of Halifax to provide him the money for a "Humane Establishment."

Wentworth initially hoped to attract three families who would settle on Sable Island at their own expense. The governing council had approved a minimal budget, and stocking the island with provisions for the shipwrecked and building the necessary structures allowed no money for salaries. No one volunteered.

Wentworth went back to the drawing board. He asked the Nova Scotia legislature to appoint five commissioners to hire a superintendent and oversee the management of the island. Then he asked for 1500 pounds start-up funding, and an annual budget of 900 pounds, plus 1000 pounds for provisions. Instead, he was granted a budget of 600 pounds that was to cover construction, wagons, clothing, relief supplies, livestock, and salaries for six men. The superintendent would receive 200 pounds annually, and each of the men would be paid 50 pounds.

Wentworth approached the Home Colonial Office at Whitehall for the remaining funds, but they would only agree to table the request "for mature consideration." He was going to have to rely on money from salvage operations to offset the expenses of running the Sable Island Lifesaving Establishment (SILE).

In 1801, the commissioners advertised a job opening for the position of superintendent of the SILE. They were looking for someone who could combine the "supreme authority of a Man of War, with the provident, paternal, and just attributes of a Supreme Magistrate or Father of a Family." The job was to be all encompassing. Not only would the superintendent be responsible for the behaviour of everybody on the island, he would also be the supreme authority in upholding all the regulations of the Humane Service.

Surprisingly, the commissioners found an excellent candidate.

Chapter 7
The Superintendent: James Morris

James Morris answered the call. He seemed to have all the right qualifications: 14 years as a navigator with the navy, skill with mechanical apparatuses, and a reputation for enterprise and hard work. His father had been the first surveyor general of Nova Scotia; his brother, Charles Junior, had been the second, and was appointed one of the commissioners of Sable Island. Wentworth judged that Morris would run a tight ship, and he was impressed with his candidate's proposal for the SILE headquarters — a pre-fabricated light-frame house that could be transported to the island on the government cutter and assembled on the sand. But, at 51, Morris was not a young man, and the post was to prove arduous.

On October 6, 1801, Morris and his entourage left Halifax for Sable Island on two ships: the brigantine *Earl of*

Moira and the schooner *Hannah*. They had with them seven months' worth of provisions; building materials; livestock — two young cows with calf, a three-year-old bull, two young sows, a boar, two rams, eight ewes, a male and female goat, and a workhorse; a supply of garden seed, nails, tools, and medicine chest; and a whaleboat with oars. Instead of the six staff that had been recommended, Morris had instead his wife and her servant, his two children, and four men: Adam Moore, David Ross, James McLaughlin, and an apprentice named John Myers. Each of them had sworn an oath to "remain upon said island, until the 1st day of May next, or until a vessel shall arrive from Halifax with orders from the Commissioners to relieve us."

The seas were rough, and it took five days for a journey that generally took only two. On reaching Sable Island, they anchored two leagues off the northwest bar to avoid being driven up onto the beach, and then strong west to northwest gales interfered with the unloading of supplies so that it took them another four days. The process was laborious — everything had to be transferred to the whaleboat and then transported to shore, the boat drawn up on the beach each time so as not to be sucked back out into the waves. Then, the men rowed the whaleboat back to the ships, loaded her up again, and returned to shore. Morris's first action as superintendent was to hire Patrick King to work on the crew.

Choosing a site near Lake Wallace, the group set up the tents that would be their only shelter until the buildings were completed. Then they transported the provisions from the beach to the settlement site. Morris had begun the guardian-ship of Sable Island that has continued uninterrupted since his arrival.

The weather was dreadful. Morris recorded in his journal that on October 15, 1801, they "suffered strong gales from the south with rain." On the 16th, they faced "storms with squalls of rain" and "fresh gales with some rain on the 17th." On October 21, under "fresh gales from the westward with squalls of rain," they raised the frame of the house. It was a disappointment. Wrote Morris: "Some parts being lost and others misnumbered, which occasioned a murmuring against the Carpenters — who must have been in Love or Stupid to have made such a Mess."

On October 22, they boarded the roof and west wall. The next day, the weather worsened, and they had great difficulty boarding the remaining walls and placing the windows. On the 24th, the wind shifted to the northwest and the men had to build cross-braces to prevent the house from collapsing. They worked steadily, boarding and then shingling the house. When they ran out of shingles, they battened with boards. They tarred the roof, hung the doors and windows, and then feasted on clams swept up on the beach. The next day, they laid the floors and cased the windows. So far they'd had no shipwrecks to contend with, but it was almost November and they were still living in tents.

On November 1, Morris finally had an opportunity to explore the island on horseback. His horse, Jolly, became mired up to his hindquarters in quicksand but was able to wrench himself free. Morris rode through a valley of cranberry and found an old shack with a supply of dried codfish ready for shipwreck survivors. Then he rode on to a high area, 366 metres from the beginning of the northeast bar, where he had arranged to meet the others. With some ceremony, they set a flagstaff, attached a box containing a map and directions to the settlement, and hoisted a blue flag. The Sable Island Lifesaving Establishment was open for business.

On November 7, the men placed a second flagstaff at the Main Station. There were no trees on Sable Island and they'd had to bring the 15-metre spruce pole with them. On November 9, they put in three tons of hay. Their life was hard. The wind made working conditions almost intolerable, and the blowing sand got into everything — their food, their clothing, even the medicine chest. When Morris's eyes became inflamed, he would stoop over a smoking fire until they watered and rinsed the grains out.

Though the weather was often terrible, Morris and his crew found no evidence of fresh shipwreck. Then one day, his dog brought home a rat. It was the first rat that Morris had seen on Sable, yet he knew logically that an island of shipwrecks would necessarily be an island of rats. Many rodents would drown when the ships broke up in the surf, but any ship that made it onto the beach would unload a cargo of not just people, but rats and mice. Indeed, he had seen plenty of mice since his arrival on the island. The cats and dogs hunted them, brought them to the house, and played with their corpses.

The Superintendent: James Morris

Morris continued his preparations. He dug wells, but found that fresh water was readily available almost anywhere on the island by digging down one metre. The water was brown but surprisingly good. He started a foundation for a barn, sowed grass seed, and built a boat they could use on Lake Wallace, where fish was plentiful. Morris and his men often used the lake to travel down the island — it was faster than walking the same distance over the sand.

The crew broke up the wrecked *Packet* for salvage, using her planks for the barn and her mast to make pickets for the garden. They built a chicken coop and a stable. When Morris ran out of shingling nails, he built a nail-making machine and turned out 5000 nails a day.

The wind was constant — only seeming to increase or decrease, to change direction, but never to cease entirely. On December 6, Morris wrote, "the Island appears to labor hard to resist the powerful Sea on all sides." Then, on Wednesday, December 16, 1801, the first of the shipwrecks occurred. It was to be an indication of what was ahead.

The *Hannah and Eliza* carried a cargo of salt from Lisbon to Boston for the cod fishery. Like so many others before him, Captain William Burrows thought himself well away from Sable Island. Instead, he sailed right into her south shore. The crew of 13 abandoned ship, launched two dinghies, and made it safely to shore.

The men were wet, exhausted, and at risk of hypothermia. They moved east along the shore, then cut inland at a break in the dunes and found a sheltered valley. They returned to the ship to salvage food and provisions and carried what they could back to their campsite. They made a tent from one of the sails, weighting the sides down with casks of bread. Then they crawled inside and tried to sleep.

In the morning, the men considered their predicament, reluctant to leave the relative warmth of their tent. Outside, the west–northwest wind carried the promise of rain. Suddenly, they heard a voice. Peering out of the tent, they saw a man approach them on horseback. The SILE had its first customers.

Morris led the crew to the halfway house, located on the north shore of the lake, 13 kilometres from Morris's own home. The halfway house was little more than a shelter, 5.5 metres × 7.3 metres, built by some earlier island resident, but now barely weatherproof. Captain Burrows and his servant lodged with the Morris family. For days, the island men and the crew of the *Hannah and Eliza* worked to salvage as much as possible from the wrecked ship. They removed the rigging, spars, cables, and cook stove. Then they improved the condition of the halfway house, waterproofing the roof with sails and caulking the walls. They cut grass for bedding and built a fireplace, for Morris had learned quickly that the salt in the driftwood ate away at the metal lining of the stoves.

Morris had made what preparations he could, but he knew that even with rationing, they would not have enough food to carry them all through to the arrival of the government schooner in May. He knew he and Captain Burrows would have to adapt one of the ship's longboats so that it could be sailed to the mainland. First they would bring it to the Main Station, then they would lengthen it and deck it over.

They gathered the carpentry tools from the SILE and the ship. The longboat was new and sturdy, and it was with some trepidation that Morris and Burrows sawed it in half right across the middle. They rebuilt the vessel, first adding a six-foot (1.8 m) keel, then planking an inner hull and an outer skeleton to make the boat longer and stronger. They caulked the planks with oakum and old rope. By mid-February, they had added the top timbers. Then they laid the main deck, caulked the seams, and waterproofed the boat with canvas and hot pitch. Finally, they built a quarterdeck, hung the rudder, placed the mast, painted the boat, and put sacks of Sable sand in the hull for ballast. Morris and Burrows had transformed the 7- × 19-foot open longboat into an 8.9- × 27-foot, two-masted decked sailing vessel. They pondered what to call her. The *Hazard* seemed appropriate.

On April 3, 1802, the *Hazard* set sail for the mainland. She carried Captain Burrows, seven of his men, their bedding and possessions, wood for the cook stove, and water and food for 15 days. Morris gave Burrows a letter for the commissioners.

Morris's report was full of praise for the work of the crew of the SILE. He "feared that their ambition would exceed their strength and consequently lead them on to death." But he did not deny the hardships. They needed more men. They could shelter people with the staff and equipment they had, but could not possibly attempt any rescue. They also needed more provisions. The men were at risk of contracting scurvy, and the rats were eating their food supply. Morris asked the commissioners to send cats in hopes of controlling the rats. In the meantime, he would experiment with building a better rat-trap.

Morris demonstrated great ingenuity in making do with inadequate supplies. That skill was going to be sorely tested in future superintendents.

Chapter 8
The Host:
Edward Hodgeson

On October 29, 1809, James Morris died on Sable Island. Under his leadership, the SILE had saved the crews and passengers of 15 ships, but the hardships of the work had destroyed his health. His second-in-command, Edward Hodgeson, who had worked with the SILE since 1804, became the next superintendent and held the post for 21 years.

The lifesaving establishment was a way of life for Edward Hodgeson and his family. Three of Edward's sons — William, James, and George — worked on the lifesaving crew, and two more would join when they were old enough. But when a ship wrecked on Sable Island, everybody assisted. In 1825 and 1826, they would be hard-pressed to keep up with the number of people they hosted, despite the number of buildings and shelters erected by

Hodgeson following detailed plans and diagrams left to him by Morris.

The trouble began with the wreck of the English brig *Adelphi*, loaded with lumber from Saint John, New Brunswick, and on her way to Liverpool, England. On September 10, 1825, she ran aground on the south shore. Fourteen people, including the captain and his wife and child, sought refuge at the establishment.

A week later, the fishing schooner *Union of Plymouth* ran aground on the northwest bar, and the Hodgesons had eight additional people to feed and shelter. They weren't overly concerned, because the government brig *Chebucto* was scheduled to arrive soon with a load of lumber, provisions, and two carpenters and could transport the castaways to Halifax on her return trip. But when the *Chebucto* arrived at Sable Island six days later, the wind had risen and the brig had to anchor several kilometres out to avoid being driven up on the beach.

Hodgeson needed the supplies. He also needed to be rid of the 22 extra people living at the settlement. He convinced the *Chebucto*'s captain, Edward Potter, to remain at anchor long enough for him to transport the castaways to the brig. It took the SILE crew three hours, taking a few people out each trip. On each return trip, Hodgeson transferred some provisions, but he knew that he was going to be short. Hodgeson was worried, but he would have been horrified if he'd known what the New Year would bring.

On the night of January 23, 1826, the Newfoundland

fishing schooner *Brothers* drove into the north shore of Sable Island. The seas were too rough for the crew to reach the beach that night. In the morning, they had no choice but to try, for the ship was breaking up. Captain McHarron and six of his men made it to shore, one of them carrying a one-year-old child. But two other crewmembers and a young woman passenger were bowled over by the surf and disappeared. The Hodgesons now had eight guests, one of them an infant.

A month later, on February 27, 1826, the *Elizabeth*, carrying a load of lumber to London, ran aground on the southeast shore during a snowstorm. The crew lowered a longboat only to watch it dash to pieces against the hull of their ship. They lowered the second longboat, but this one upset and was smashed by the surf. Afraid to risk losing their last boat, they decided to wait until morning in hopes that the weather would clear.

They waited 24 hours before making a third and successful attempt. Hodgeson and his men had been stationed on the beach, ready to assist them, in conditions far worse than those on board the ship. With the captain and the crew of 18, Hodgeson (now seriously ill after 24 hours on the beach) had 27 survivors in his care. Though he'd been able to salvage some provisions from the *Elizabeth*, he knew he didn't have sufficient quantities to feed 27 additional people until spring.

So again, the SILE crew constructed a boat from salvage. It took them five weeks, but on Wednesday, April 5, 1826, the captains and three crewmembers from each vessel set sail for

Halifax. By the following Monday, the *Chebucto* was on her way to pick up the remaining 19 castaways. Hodgeson had suffered the onslaught well enough, but he was in for more.

On April 27, the brig *Traveller*, loaded with salt and on her way to Halifax from Liverpool, grounded on the outer end of the northeast bar. Fourteen people made their way to Hodgeson's shelter. Captain Penrice and his crew immediately began to construct a boat. It was well he did, for another ship would soon wreck.

The *Nassau* was an emigrant ship from Ireland, bound for Quebec City. On May 13, 1826, she stranded on the northwest bar, as had the *Traveller*. But the *Nassau* was farther out on the bar, at much higher risk of breaking up before the men could get to her. The lifesaving crew, assisted by some of the crew of the *Traveller*, headed out as far as they could on the west point, hoping to see a longboat heading to shore. They were relieved when they saw not one, but two of them, but they were still kilometres out. It would be several hours before they reached shore.

The longboats came close. The first, timing its arrival with the waves, went right up onto the beach. The second boat stove on the beach, breaking up before the lifesaving crew and hurling the passengers into the water. The SILE men leaped to the rescue, but were unable to save seven people — five men and two women. Even with this loss, 37 castaways made it safely to shore and needed housing, food, and warm clothing. Hodgeson had one of his children take them to the Main Station while he remained and planned for the rescue of the people still on board the *Nassau*. He had lived on Sable Island for 25 years and knew that the *Nassau* was unlikely to hold together much longer.

The next day, the sea was so high that they could do nothing but pray for the men, women, and children still aboard. Hodgeson was not going to risk the lives of his own crew in a fruitless and foolish attempt at rescue. But the following morning, the weather cleared and Captain Penrice of the *Traveller* set off for Halifax with six of his crew and a letter from William Hodgeson requesting assistance. The lifesaving crew then headed out to the *Nassau*.

It was an arduous rescue. It was eight miles (13 km) to the *Nassau*, and eight miles (13 km) back with the fully loaded whaler. The passengers were of little help, afraid to get into the whaler, but more afraid of being left behind. When they approached the beach, the men synchronized their rowing with the action of the waves so as to benefit from their lift without being crushed by them. As soon as the first group of survivors was unloaded, the men immediately turned the whaler back toward the sea, pushed her off, jumped in, and rowed the eight miles (13 km) back to the *Nassau*.

By the end of the day, they had rescued an additional 80 people. This brought the number in Hodgeson's care to 123. He hoped mightily that Captain Penrice would make it to Halifax with the letter. With luck, he would reach the mainland the next day and the cutter would arrive at the island a few days later. Hodgeson judged that he had enough supplies to last him until then. He could always slaughter a cow or shoot a horse, although he'd found that people were fussy about eating horsemeat.

Then, on June 2, 1826, with still no word from Halifax, the unbelievable happened — the *Agamemnon*, loaded with timber for Glasgow, Scotland, struck Sable Island. Hodgeson had another 18 survivors under his care, bringing the number of people receiving his hospitality to 141 men, women, and children.

The relief schooner finally arrived to find far more shipwrecked passengers than had been expected. Captain Penrice had estimated the number aboard the *Nassau*, but he had sailed before the *Agamemnon* had capsized.

The men of the establishment were praised for their bravery and determination. But 20 years later, a different SILE crew would witness a rescue that would have amazed even Hodgeson and his men.

Chapter 9
The Sea Captain:
Captain Higgins

On September 19, 1846, Captain Higgins and his crew of 12 fished the Banquero Bank, southeast of Sable Island. It was the richest of the banks, but if the weather turned foul, boats there had to sail past Sable Island to reach an American or Canadian harbour.

The weather had been fine that morning, with a light breeze from the east. The sky was clear, not a cloud to be seen, but there was a tinge to it, a heaviness like pewter. The seas ran high, far too high considering the lack of wind. Higgins knew what that meant. There was a gale coming his way. He was ahead of it, but it would reach him, of that he had no doubt. He rang the bell to call the dories back to the *Arno* and soon set sail for the mainland.

At noon, the sky seemed to dull even further — it was

the colour of lead. The wind increased to a fresh breeze from due east, and the ocean took on phosphorescence. As each wave peaked, it looked as if someone had taken a paintbrush dipped in shimmer and curled it here and there over the waves. Higgins recognized it for what it was — a pre-hurricane sea.

At midnight, the watch reported heavy gales from the east to northeast, with rain from the northeast. Sometime during the night, they lost their headsails. They were at the mercy of the storm now, barely able to manoeuvre, the ship unbalanced and difficult to control. At dawn, the wind veered to north–northeast and Higgins saw Sable Island dead ahead. They had been caught in Sable's currents, the ones that take a ship from the south side of the island to the north side, and back again. A body drowned off Sable might travel for days circling round and round the island until it either sank or was taken by the sharks.

Higgins dropped anchor in 20 fathoms of water. He paid out 300 fathoms of hemp cable, and the *Arno* turned into the wind. They would try to ride out the storm.

By noon, Higgins knew that the gale would not blow itself out before his ship foundered in the waves. He had a choice. He could cut the cable, turn the *Arno* towards Sable Island, and run her on shore before dark, or he could wait for the sea to take them to her depths.

Higgins ordered his men to cut the cable and hoist and close-reef the mainsail. There was no point wasting time hauling anchor. He knew there would be little left of the schooner, whichever choice he made. But one choice offered him the chance to save his men. Higgins planned to run the schooner before the wind. But first, he had to prepare the ship. He was an experienced sea captain, and in his travels, he had heard tales of pouring oil on troubled waters. He explained his plan to the crew.

Two men were to stay on deck; the rest were to go below and pray for their survival. Higgins nailed the cabin doors shut behind them. The waves would soon be of such ferocity that cabin doors would be torn right off their frames if they weren't nailed tightly down. Then, he and the two men placed two large casks of fish oil and blubber near the fore shrouds and lashed them in place. Next, Higgins tied the men to the casks. Then he tied a wooden ladle to the outer arm of each man, for if the ladle was lost, so was the schooner. The men were disbelieving. Fish oil seemed an unlikely saviour to them.

In fact, the use of fish oil was well known — it had even appeared in Lloyd's Calendar under the title "use of oil in Modifying the Effects of Breaking Waves." Not much oil was needed to coat the water and prevent the waves from breaking. Still, Higgins was concerned. He knew the oil was effective on "free waves," those in deep water, but its value in surf, or where waves break from the bottom, was less certain. The *Arno* had to pass through the surf if he was to save his crew.

The wind was directly behind them now. Higgins told the men to wait for his signal, for they couldn't use the oil too soon or they would have none left when it was most needed. At his sign, they were to dip their ladles into the fish oil and then fling the oil up into the air as high as they could. The wind would carry the oil forward and coat the water. The men had only to keep ladling, timing their flinging of the oil with the rush of the waves so that the oil's effect was not wasted. Higgins then lashed himself to the helm, hoping that the ship would hold together to reach Sable's shores.

Three miles (4.8 km) from the beach, Higgins gave his signal. The effect of the oil was immediate. Although the waves rose like mountains on either side of the *Arno*, their curled crests reaching as high as the top of her masts, they did not touch her. The sea remained smooth before the ship — it rolled under her rather than battering her with a force that tore everything loose. The schooner met each wave as if destruction were imminent, but then sailed smoothly through and onto the next wave.

They were a mile (1.6 km) out now, just approaching the island's outer bar, where every sea breaks from the bottom. This would be the ultimate test. Higgins tensed. Sometimes the oil worked; sometimes it was unable to calm the surf. The schooner passed through undamaged, her wake a shining trail of oil-coated water. Another half mile (0.8 km) and she shuddered onto the outer beach.

The island's current superintendent, Joseph Darby, and his men were ready. They had watched the schooner since dawn, cheering her progress. Now, they extended a rope from an anchor in the sand down to the vessel's bow. Hanging on to this lifeline so that they would not be swept into the sea, they made their way out to the *Arno*. Higgins untied himself and his two crewmen, and they wrenched open the cabin doors. One by one, the crewmembers lowered themselves from the *Arno* into the arms of the men of the SILE.

The crew of the *Arno* had not enough words to express their gratitude to Superintendent Darby and his men. They had heard of Darby's heroic rescues, of the medals he had been awarded. Soon they would be hearing more about his failures than his successes.

Chapter 10
The Imperfect Hero: Joseph Darby

oseph Darby, the third superintendent of Sable Island, had served on the lifesaving crew under both previous superintendents. The commissioners were delighted to have him, for he was a hero on both sides of the Atlantic and had brought positive publicity to the SILE.

His first heroic rescue had taken place eight years before his appointment as superintendent. In May 1822, Darby, then captain of the *Two Brothers*, the government vessel that transported provisions to Sable Island, was making his approach to the island from the northwest when he glanced over the sand bar to the south side of the island. Amazingly, a vessel had run aground about a kilometre offshore.

Darby considered his position. He could go around the northwest bar to reach the vessel, but that route was at least

16 kilometres long. He knew from his earlier service with the SILE that a channel cut through the bar just beyond the west point. If he passed through that, he'd save a lot of time. Thankfully, the *Two Brothers* had a shallow draught, but nevertheless, Darby knew that if he miscalculated, he could add his ship to the list of those wrecked on the northwest bar.

Darby changed course and headed through the gap. He watched the crew on the wrecked frigate *Africaine* lower boats to the water and attempt to make their way to the beach. But the crew was ill prepared for the surf, and several of the boats upset. Darby saw that Superintendent Hodgeson and his men had been able to rescue some of the capsized men and drag them to safety.

He estimated there were 70 sailors on the beach. Darby knew that a frigate the size of the *Africaine* would carry more than 200 men. There was not enough time to make the many trips that would be required to remove the rest of the crew. Darby made a snap decision. He ordered his men to jettison the *Two Brothers'* cargo, starting with the lumber. The establishment was going to have to wait another six months for the new halfway house.

Darby eased the *Two Brothers* close to the frigate. He signalled Captain Epron to prepare his men to transfer to the government schooner. It would be hazardous in the rough seas, but Darby knew it would be safer than risking their lives in the longboats. He also knew that the *Africaine* was in danger of breaking up. He didn't have much time for the transfer.

Closer still he came, and the men of each ship threw

lines to the other, to keep the ships side-by-side. Then the men of the frigate jumped onto the government ship and moved to the far side of the deck to make room for the rest. When everyone was off the frigate, Darby swung his ship around and navigated his way back through the channel to the calmer waters of the north side. He anchored offshore and began the laborious transfer of the men from the ship to land.

Two days later, Darby arrived in Halifax with 7 officers and 130 seamen. As soon as they had disembarked, Governor Sir James Kempt ordered Darby to return to Sable Island with replacement provisions and a new supply of lumber, and to bring back the remainder of the *Africaine*'s seamen.

When Captain Epron returned to France, he told King Louis-Philippe of Darby's valour and skill, and of the assistance of the SILE. The king decided that nothing less than a medal should reward such bravery and devotion to duty, and he awarded gold medals to Darby and Hodgeson, together with a reward of 94 pounds sterling each. Two of the SILE crew were awarded a gratuity.

As superintendent, Darby would be awarded a second gold medal in May 1840, for the rescue of 80 people from the French vessel *Maria*. Her master, Captain Born, wrote in his testimonial of the "fearlessness and devotion to duty of Captain Darby and his crew," praising "these brave mariners who in order to save us have so many times imperilled their lives." That event marked the high point of Darby's career, before his fall from favour.

The SILE had grown under Darby's leadership. There

were now two inhabited outposts on the eastern end of the island, one at the east end of Lake Wallace, and another 4.8 kilometres west of the east point. A mounted patrol using the Sable Island horses checked the entire island regularly.

Darby had a crew of seven men, including one of his sons and one of Hodgeson's. Each was paid 50 shillings a month, or about $140 a year, and was to receive an additional 20 shillings for every wreck that they salvaged. The work was gruelling, the rewards few, and the provisions were dispersed in a manner that seemed like rationing rather than the allotment of daily requirements.

Darby controlled virtually every aspect of life on Sable Island. He recorded everything in his journal. "I gave Adams, keeper of the eastern outpost three and a half pounds of tea and he says that he cannot make three pounds last him three months. I gave him nine pounds of coffee, two gallons molasses, 25 pounds of sugar, some rice, barley, oatmeal, dry fish, powder, shot, and peas." Adams, like the others, was supposed to supplement his diet with produce from his own garden.

But Darby became abusive of the men. In August 1847, a new recruit named Robert Nichols sent a letter to the commissioners via the government supply ship complaining of "diabolical proceedings and dishonesty of the present Superintendent of Sable Island." Nichols told of being stationed all night on the beach, of being soaking wet for hours at a time, so that he was covered in "festering sores and painful boils."

In truth, the working conditions were no worse than they had been for any other member of the SILE. The difference was that Darby threatened to flog Nichols when he said he was too sick to work. Nichols beseeched the commissioners to investigate the management of the SILE. A bright new political light would do just that.

In 1848, Nova Scotia elected a Reform government. The provincial secretary was Joseph Howe, son of John Howe, who had authored the original Sable Island report for Governor Wentworth. It seemed to the younger Howe that the island that had once been overrun by wreckers, pirates, and other scoundrels was now being run by an equally ruthless person, and the government was paying him a salary to do it. Stories about Joseph Darby were circulating in Halifax — stories that spoke of bravery, certainly, but also of embezzlement, fraud, and abuse.

Joseph Howe set off for the island on a personal inspection and assigned Captain W. T. Townsend to conduct a formal inquiry. Townsend's report so alarmed Howe that he forwarded it to a committee of the executive council so they could investigate "the whole condition of the Establishment."

The committee made nine allegations against Superintendent Darby. The first was of "general severity and harshness of manner towards people on the island." The second dealt with his treatment of Nichols, which was so harsh that they felt it needed to be addressed separately from the first allegation.

The next charge was that Darby profited from accepting people on the island who were a source of embarrassment to their family. Moneyed people in Nova Scotia sent alcoholics and "insane people" to the island, sometimes for a cure, other times for anonymity.

The fourth charge was that Darby showed a lack of respect to the commissioners; the fifth was that he sold liquor to the settlement staff in violation of the Sable Island regulation prohibiting alcohol. Darby had been reprimanded for this same activity in 1836.

The charges continued. It was alleged that Darby charged castaways for cooking and other services provided, and accepted both cash and clothes for these services. It was said he had put his 11-year-old son on the payroll as cook, claiming both salary and bonuses for wrecks for him, under a fictitious name.

The commissioners went on to accuse Darby of not only stocking his eldest son's vessel from SILE supplies, but of selling SILE supplies to visiting ships, without recording those sales in the island accounts. The final charge was that Darby used his position as superintendent to promote the interests of his family.

The public was intrigued. A March 1849 editorial in the *Halifax Times and Courier* clearly came out on the side of Joseph Darby. If he were truly so bad at his job, wouldn't the commissioners have noticed? In reality, the commissioners had visited Sable Island on only a few occasions since 1801, and never for more than the time it took to unload the government supply ship.

Darby's defence was a wonder of rationalization and invention. In answer to the first charge brought by the inquiry,

Darby stated that he never asked of his men more than he was prepared to do himself. If they couldn't follow him, they were "not fit for the service." As for his treatment of Nichols, well, "any accusation of ill-treatment was utterly false," said Darby. "He had plenty to eat, and done nothing but sleep and walk about and look for himself."

The charge that Darby had received payment for accepting insane people on the island caused a furore. While two of the people were no longer living on Sable Island, the third, a Mr. Etter, had been there for 17 years. Mr. Etter was a "man of respectable family, heir to some property, and his guardians of the highest standing in the community." Darby made it clear that Michael Wallace, one of the commissioners, had approved his acceptance of the man, had listed him on the SILE accounts as a schoolteacher, and even paid him a salary.

Darby would have done well to keep silent, but he added that they'd had to confine Mr. Etter at night, and that it was difficult to make any place strong enough to contain him. If they didn't confine him, he cut away boats and set them adrift, broke windows, and was generally violent. Darby readily admitted that very harsh measures had been used with Etter, but stated that now the man was "quiet and inoffensive" and "was usefully employed carrying wood and water."

Darby was entirely unapologetic regarding the charge that he was disrespectful towards the commissioners. His frustration at their poor management of the SILE mirrored that of Morris and Hodgeson. Commissioners had ignored the island, he said. They never gave him notice of scheduled visits, so he never knew when he might get relief from caring for castaways. In 1846, he'd had 80 to 90 castaways in his care for up to three months. His wife, who by the way, he said, was not paid a salary by the commission, had had to bake 90 pounds of bread a day to feed the people. Darby argued that far from being disrespectful, it was his job to point out the weaknesses in the commissioners' work.

As to the charge of selling liquor, he had been acquitted of that in 1836 and expected to be acquitted again. He did not deny that he'd done it on a very small scale, but only "for the benefit of the people ... and it was a great pleasure to the Superintendent to do any kindness to good men."

And so the hearings continued. Yes, his son received a salary as cook, but the commissioners would not pay his wife to cook, and none of the men would cook, feeling that the "duties of a cook were obnoxious duties for a man to be confined to."

Darby was raging now. Years of frustration with the commission's poor management, and years of doing without necessary provisions, made him fearless. He was unapologetic and unrepentant.

He wrote a letter to the editor of the *Halifax Times and Courier*, furious that the commissioners had accused him of thinking of himself as a commander of a man-of-war. "A commander would have put Nichols in irons," he proclaimed, and a commander wouldn't have tolerated such criticisms as he, Darby, had suffered. He argued that he had been paid at a rate slightly higher than that of a schoolteacher or a skilled farm hand, nowhere near the salary of a captain of a man-of-war. "It would be a disgrace to any captain of a man-of-war to compare him with the poor, despised, over-wrought Superintendent of the Wrecking Establishment on Sable Island." Darby then claimed that he had performed more important and more difficult feats during his time as superintendent than any two captains of a man-of-war may have performed during the same period.

Halifax was a town of navy men and naval tradition. They didn't appreciate this man comparing himself favourably to the highest-ranked captain in the British Navy. Darby ran a salvage operation and a lifesaving station — hardly the stuff of battles.

The Board of Inquiry brought down its decision, and Darby was fired from his position as superintendent. On November 8, 1848, he and his family boarded the government vessel for the last time. Unfortunately, his disgrace received more press coverage than his justified criticisms of the inadequate equipment provided to the lifesaving establishment. It would be a woman who would bring the world's attention to this need.

Chapter 11
The Samaritan: Dorothea Lynde Dix

Dorothea Lynde Dix was 12 years old when she ran away from her parents' home in Hampden, Maine, and travelled alone to her grandmother's in Boston. The same independence that enabled her to run away showed itself again when she graduated from school. Dorothea wanted to be a teacher, but not just any teacher. She wanted to have her own school, wanted to run it the way she thought schools should be run, and wanted children to be treated with respect and compassion. It was her commitment to humanity, and a chance meeting, that would later bring the SILE to her attention.

As planned, Dorothea established her own school, and she worked hard at her vocation until exhaustion defeated her. Then, while she was still recovering, her grandmother died and Dorothea inherited a great deal of money. She eventually returned to teaching, but not to her school. Instead, she went to the Boston jail and volunteered to teach the inmates. It was a pivotal decision for her. She had never been exposed to the appalling conditions inside a jail. What she witnessed, especially the degradation of those who were mentally ill, changed the focus of her work. Dorothea became a reformer, and a reformer with clout and connections.

Dorothea first tried to improve conditions for the inmates. She was unsuccessful, but did manage to have the Boston jailer charged. She then lobbied state legislatures to improve conditions for the mentally ill across the country. Dissatisfied with their efforts, she founded asylums where the patients would be treated with compassion, not degradation.

In the summer of 1853, Dorothea expanded her interest to include Canadian institutions and visited St. John's, Newfoundland. During her stay, massive gales caused huge destruction in the town and loss of life among the fishermen. Dorothea was profoundly impacted by what she witnessed, and the loss of so many lives weighed heavily on her as she made her way to Halifax for the next part of her journey. She had arranged to meet with the Honourable Hugh Bell, mayor of the city, to discuss founding an asylum in Halifax. Bell had written to Dorothea of the terrible conditions at the poorhouse. He told her that he had seen 47 patients housed in a ward of only 18 beds, and that some patients were kept naked and chained to the floor.

Bell also happened to have responsibility for Sable Island. After the Darby inquiry, administration of the SILE was transferred to the Board of Works, of which Bell was chairman. He told Dorothea about Mr. Etter, and of how he understood why the family would choose to send him to Sable Island rather than subject him to the horrors of the poorhouse.

Talk of Sable Island turned to the work of the lifesaving crew, and Dorothea, fresh from the dreadful tragedy in Newfoundland, asked if she could talk with the crewmembers of the establishment. On July 26, 1853, she and Bell travelled to Sable Island on the supply ship *Daring*. Two days into their stay, the schooner *Guide*, en route from New York to Labrador, ran aground on the sand bar off the south shore. Like so many before him, Captain Henry Millichamp was unaware of his proximity to Sable Island. Travelling under full sail in a thick fog, he hit the bar with immense force.

Dorothea mounted one of the Sable Island horses and rode to the beach to witness the rescue. She watched the men struggle to bring the heavy surfboat from the Main Station, watched as they launched the boat into the turbulent water and rowed out to the wreck. For hours they went back and forth, straining at the oars, soaked by the waves, their hands bleeding from the friction of the salt and the sand. They rescued the crew and went back for the captain. Then they returned to the schooner to unload the cargo before the ship disintegrated.

Dorothea left Sable Island that evening impressed by the courage and determination of the lifesaving crew, but horrified at the conditions under which they worked, and at the notion that they were expected to risk their lives to salvage cargo. Determined to do something to improve the lot of the SILE, she contacted Robert B. Forbes, chairman of the Boston Humane Society — an agency whose job it was to save lives at sea. Dorothea described to Forbes in vivid detail what she had witnessed during the rescue. She told him of the difficulty the crew had faced in handling the boats and explained that Sable Island's unique topography meant the men often had to travel kilometres to even approach a wreck. She then asked Forbes to compile a list of the best equipment to meet the needs of the SILE crew. She would take care of raising the money to pay for it.

Next, Dorothea approached her moneyed friends in Boston, New York, and Philadelphia, and in less than five months had raised enough money to purchase lifeboats — not the heavy wooden ones that the SILE crew was currently using, but lighter, metal ones with double hulls and one-way scupper drains that emptied the boat when water washed in over the gunwales. The boats were more buoyant and, in tests, could safely carry 60 adult men.

Dorothea took pleasure in naming the new lifeboats after the cities that had raised the funds: The *Victoria* of Boston, the *Grace Darling* of Philadelphia, and the *Reliance* and *Samaritan* of New York. With the remaining money, she purchased cables and harnesses, as well as a life-car and mortar apparatus for firing a lifeline to a stranded vessel and bringing people to shore.

Getting the lifeboats to Sable Island proved more difficult than Dorothea had imagined. The sponsors wanted publicity for their generosity, and for months the lifeboats sat in display windows on Wall Street. Eventually, Dorothea insisted that they be transported to Sable Island. But the transport vessel wrecked on the American coast and the lifeboats were damaged. Dorothea had them shipped back to New York, determined that they be in perfect condition when they arrived on Sable Island.

It would be another 11 months before the lifeboats reached the SILE. Sixteen days after their arrival, on November 27, 1854, the *Reliance* proved her worth.

That morning, James Farquahar, keeper of the East End Station, observed flotsam on the surf when he made his morning patrol on Old Sam. He urged the horse on faster and saw the wreck 183 metres out on the south side of the northeast bar. She was the biggest ship that Farquahar had ever seen, and he had seen enough wrecks to know that, big as she was, she was also in trouble. Both her main and mizzenmasts were gone, and she listed to seaward. Farquahar saw the crew and passengers huddled in the forecastle, or high in the rigging, trying to get beyond the reach of the tremendous waves.

Farquahar hurried back to his station and sent his son to ride the 19 kilometres to the Main Station to raise the alarm. He knew the lifesaving crew would have to row the *Reliance* almost 26 kilometres to get to the wreck. He estimated that it might be six hours before they arrived.

The 715-ton *Arcadia* had already spent one night on the bar, and every man, woman, and child watched as the *Reliance* approached. But the seas and current were stronger than the crew had anticipated, and the *Reliance* swept past. The men continued on to the beach, where they dragged up the lifeboat well windward of the *Arcadia* and launched her again. At 3 p.m., she finally reached the stuck vessel and took on her first load of people.

The SILE crew was anxious. They had only two hours of daylight left to them, but they didn't want to panic the passengers and have them all try to get off the ship at the same time. They rowed the *Reliance* to shore, unloaded the castaways, and returned to the *Arcadia*.

Four more times they made the return trip through waves and currents that tried to carry the rescue boat along the bar. Then it was dark, and the rescue had to be halted for the night. The men of the SILE had saved 80 people, but they knew another 83 remained on the ship. They could do no more that night, so they pulled the *Reliance* high up the beach, away from the waterline.

The remaining passengers, seeing the *Reliance* beached on the sand, cried out to Superintendent Mathew D. McKenna. Those already rescued beseeched him to go back for their husbands, children, or wives. How long, they asked, could people survive in this cold, soaking wet as they were? How long could they maintain their hold on the rigging before their figures grew fatigued?

McKenna could do nothing for them that night, nothing but hope and pray that the ship would hold together for another 24 hours. He found the cries of the abandoned so heartrending that he couldn't bear to mount his horse in sight of them and led the horse away. When he was far enough that the roaring of the sea and the sound of the wind drowned them out, he climbed into the saddle and rode to the Main Station.

Those passengers who had been rescued were taken to the East End Station. The women with young children were settled in the house; the rest bedded down in the hay in the barn. McKenna would get no sleep that night. He needed replacement oars and tholepins, and had to ready the life-car and mortar apparatus in case the weather worsened.

At first light, the rescue team began again. They made 10 trips to the stranded vessel and back again, removing all of the passengers and crew. Then they made repeated trips to salvage the cargo, clothing, and provisions. That night, the *Arcadia* "broke into a thousand pieces," and McKenna marvelled at the destructive force of the ocean at Sable Island. The *Arcadia* had been a fine ship, built only five years earlier in Warren, Maine, yet the surf had destroyed her in less than 72 hours.

The public hailed McKenna and his crew as heroes. The superintendent believed that honour belonged elsewhere — to the *Reliance* and her benefactor, Dorothea Dix. Dorothea declined credit, and then set about bringing more benefits to Sable Island. Having noticed that there was little reading material for either the residents or the castaways on the island, she approached friends and booksellers for contributions to a library. Hundreds of books were received in time to be shipped on the next government supply ship.

Next, she lobbied the Shipwrecked Fishermen and Royal Benevolent Society in England for recognition of McKenna and his staff amongst their peers in other lifesaving establishments. She wanted the men of the SILE to have real evidence that their "services in a lonely and desolate land are honorably estimated and gratefully recorded." She was successful, and the society awarded a gold medal to McKenna and silver medals to his crew.

A quarter of a century later, a castaway would keep a diary of her own shipwreck on Sable Island, recording for posterity the work of the SILE.

Chapter 12
The Castaway: Janet Carnochan

Janet Carnochan was about to turn 40, a reality that reaffirmed her decision to travel to Europe. The Niagara, Ontario, teacher was no longer content telling her students about the wonders of England, France, and Italy without seeing firsthand what she described so vividly to them. On July 12, 1879, she set sail from New York on the steamer *State of Virginia*, embarking on the first leg of her European adventure.

Ever the observer, Janet jotted down notes to incorporate into her lesson plans. She had never been on a ship before, had never even seen the ocean. She inhaled the tangy salt air, so refreshing after the dust and heat of New York. She caught a whiff of manure and thought that, though the crew had done a good job of building a partition on deck to separate the cows from the passengers, the animals were making their presence known in other ways.

Janet recorded the notes from the ship's log in her journal — they had travelled 297 miles (478 km) the first day and 289 miles (465 km) the next. She recorded comments about the porpoises and whales she saw; learned how to tell the points of the compass using the north star; and recognized Cassiopeia, something of which she was inordinately proud. Rather guiltily, she made notes about her fellow travellers. There were 150 on the steamer, including crew and passengers. One of the passengers, a young widow named Mrs. Moutin, had an exquisitely beautiful two-year-old daughter, Marie, upon whom she and all the crew doted. There were two other widows, of war or disease, Janet didn't know. She was glad for them, that they each had a child. Captain Moodie had brought his daughter with him, although there was no sight of Mrs. Moodie. Then there was a peculiar man, Thomas Peden, who was travelling with his wife, Mary, and their two boys, John and Richard. In fairness, Janet didn't know whether his peculiarity predated his sunstroke, but he had been almost violent the previous day in the throes of his fever. Today's fog should have helped, she thought.

The fog whistle, sounding at short intervals, woke her several times during the night, but she easily fell asleep again. She didn't give much thought to the danger it presented. Atlantic crossings were commonplace in 1879. Some of the passengers, and even Captain Moodie, said that they had made this trip 20 to 30 times in the last six years. But she remembered a curious thing before she fell asleep.

The Castaway: Janet Carnochan

Janet had checked the ship's log earlier in the evening. As usual, it recorded longitude and latitude, but there was an addendum to the note. "Not accurate," it said. The ship's navigator had estimated that the *State of Virginia* was 25 miles (40.2 km) off Sable Island, but the fog had wrecked havoc with visual navigation aids. Janet was curious about Sable Island. She had heard of the daring of the SILE, and had followed the controversy over placing a lighthouse at such a fog-ridden location. She was rather hoping to glimpse this mysterious place.

At 7:50 p.m., a sudden jolt, and then another, showed that the navigator had indeed miscalculated and that Janet was going to make a far closer acquaintance with Sable Island than she'd intended. The ship was not 25 miles (40.2 km) from Sable Island — she had run aground on Sable Island.

Passengers rushed on deck — some were panicked, others were merely curious. The behaviour of the crew did not reassure them. Though the ship's engine still ran, crewmembers were shouting orders and rushing about with ropes and chains. "Have we hit a boat?" wondered Janet. They hadn't, but the depth sounder showed they were in 18 feet (5.5 m) of water. The *State of Virginia* required a 22-foot (6.7 m) draught.

The crew dropped anchors and put the engine into reverse, hoping to haul the ship off the sand bar. Captain Moodie didn't seem terribly alarmed. The tide would be at its peak at midnight, and he had every faith that he could float the ship off the bar. He would jettison cargo if need be, but he didn't want to do that unless absolutely essential. No captain wanted to account to owners for a loss of shipments, and the sea was calm. There was no need for panic.

A new sound changed that. Janet heard a grinding noise, a grating like metal against rocks, but she knew there were no rocks at Sable Island. Despite the anchors, the ship had swung so that she lay sideways along the bar, and the rudder chain had broken and was grating against the ship's hull. Janet did not need captain's papers to recognize that their predicament had worsened. The ship was now both stuck and crippled. Moodie in turn, realized that he now had no choice but to jettison the cargo. But there wasn't enough time to do that before the high tide at midnight. Instead, he would wait for the following high tide the next day at noon. Perhaps the Sabbath would provide a miracle.

Moodie suggested the passengers return to their berths, to sleep if possible. But the passengers were fearful of being trapped below. Some sat on deckchairs, others lay on lounges in the saloon. A few returned to their berths to pack their belongings, but immediately came above again lugging their trunks. Janet lay down at 4 a.m., but the noise of a ship beached on a sand bar was disquieting if not alarming. The timbers were creaking and grinding against the bar, and the surf was roaring in the distance. Janet couldn't see for the fog and the dark, but it sounded tumultuous. Now that the ship was beached parallel to the shore, her bow no longer cut the waves, but instead absorbed the full force of the waves against the length of her hull. Janet rose, put on two dresses and an ulster, and returned to the deck.

The Castaway: Janet Carnochan

At dawn, the captain encouraged the passengers to eat their breakfast. They would need their strength, and it gave them something to do rather than pace the deck, peering into the fog at a shore they could only hear. The crew fired the distress cannon, hoping to be heard by the SILE. The fog lifted momentarily, and Janet could see a lighthouse, indistinct through the mist, but a lighthouse nevertheless. The beach seemed much farther than she had imagined from the sound of the waves — it was at least half a mile (0.8 km) from the ship. Then the fog closed in again and shrouded everything.

When the fog lifted once more, Janet saw an incredible sight. On the shore were immense horses, giant men, a colossus of a wagon, and an enormous lifeboat — all magnified by the moisture in the air. One of the ship's lifeboats left the *State of Virginia* and headed to shore. It soon returned to the ship, followed by one of the SILE lifeboats. The master of the SILE boat gave a terse order. The captain was to land the passengers immediately, for the surf was worsening. It looked not much different to Janet, but she noticed the strained expressions on the faces of the SILE crew.

But Captain Moodie first wanted to attempt to float the ship. He ordered the crew to jettison the cargo. They tore down the barriers separating the cows from the passengers, "dragged, pushed and hauled" the animals to the side of the steamer, and shoved them overboard. Janet had assumed the cows would make for shore, but instead they circled, gazing up at the passengers. A crewmember used his boat to try to lead the cattle to land, but they ignored him, and Janet watched, horrified, as one cow and then another sank from exhaustion. Then, just when it seemed as if all would drown, the surviving animals turned abruptly and headed for the beach. The water around the ship was littered with dead cows, barrels, and crates of cheese, flour, and other provisions. Passenger and crew trunks were jettisoned next. But the *State of Virginia* still did not float off the sand.

The SILE crew insisted that the women and children be sent to shore immediately. Janet hesitated, then, at a crewmember's strong urging, allowed herself to be lowered to the lifeboat that was pitching in the water below. Ten other women and two children followed her. Pulling on the oars, the steersman in the lifeboat told them, "I will do my best to take you all ashore, but it looks bad." Janet and the others sat like stones.

The sea looked far more forbidding at this level, and for the first time, Janet realized how precarious was their situation. From the ship, the breakers looked much alike, but in their midst, Janet felt the tremendous force that carried them closer and closer to safety.

It was not a simple matter to land. Twice the crew backed from their approach, and then at a cry of "Try it now. Go on, then, in the name of God," they pulled full ahead. A wave washed over them, and then the next carried them right up onto the beach. The men of the SILE rushed out waist deep into the waves and pulled the boat higher onto the beach, so that it would not be sucked back by the next wave.

Superintendent Duncan McDonald helped the women

and children out of the lifeboat, and the crew set out again for a second load. Janet sat down on the sand to recover her strength, only to find herself attacked by terns. All around her was a sea of nests — some with eggs, others with downy hatchlings. The adult terns dove at her, their sharp bills raking her head, their shrieking relentless and piercing until she moved away.

True to the steersman's prediction, the surf worsened. From shore, Janet could see them load the second boat. There were 11 women and 5 children on board. Captain Moodie led his daughter to the ladder and watched her climb down into the lifeboat before returning to his post. As soon as his back was turned, the girl clambered up the ladder again, and the lifeboat turned for the beach and drew close to shore. As with Janet's passage, the waves lifted the lifeboat high into the air. But this time, the crew had miscalculated, or the sea had changed, and instead of being carried onto the beach, the boat was hurled end over end, its passengers flung into the water.

Immobilized with shock, Janet could see the men clinging to the upturned boat with one hand, reaching out to clutch a woman or child with the other. Then the boat righted itself and came closer to shore, and again, those on shore rushed into the water to snatch the boat and any person, whether living or dead. Janet approached the waterline. Two women lay there, the white foam on their lips witness to their drowning. Four woman and all five children were missing.

Janet's heart wrenched when she realized that little

Marie Mouton, the beautiful two-year-old blonde child, was missing, sucked into the sea. Her mother, blood pouring from her mouth, was walking aimlessly along the shore. Mrs. Widestrand, mother of a three-year-old boy, had altered almost beyond recognition, so blue and rigid were her features. Janet did what little she could, loosening the woman's dress, rubbing her back to warm her, and then wrapping her in a blanket. Another lady bled from a cut in her neck, dragged from the water by her veil. Three women, two of them widows, had each lost their only child. The wife of the sunstroke victim was gone, too, as were her two sons. And the lifeboat was stove in, beyond repair.

Janet glanced up from where she stood with Mrs. Widestrand. Two of the ship's lifeboats were drawing close. They had to be stopped, but how? The roar of the waves was thunderous and the voices of those on shore would never be heard. But the men on board the boats, seeing the agitation of the people on the island, the shaking of their heads, and the waving of their arms, turned back to the *State of Virginia*.

Janet and the other survivors were taken to the superintendent's home. No one slept that night. Those on shore wondered how their loved ones would fare on the ship. Those on the ship had no way of knowing who had survived the capsizing. During the night, the men in the lifeboats attempted but failed to find the gap in the northwest bar, then made their way back to the ship. Nothing, however, would prevail them to climb back on board. The seams in the *State of Virginia* had "started," and water was seeping into her hold.

At dawn, those in the lifeboats found the gap with no difficulty and made their way to the north shore, where the others waited for them. Janet was shocked at the men's appearance — they were unshaved and unkempt, wet to the waist, and dressed in an odd assortment of clothing. Instead of suitcases, they carried blankets, life preservers, food, and valuables.

People who had lost a loved one were taken aside. The cries were heartrending. Mr. Peden, unable to absorb the news of the loss of his entire family, walked amidst the others, asking in a monotone, "Have you seen my wife? Where is she?" He didn't wait for an answer, but went on to the next group, asking them the same questions.

A crew was chosen to travel to Halifax to raise the alarm. They loaded the best lifeboat with provisions and took with them messages to telegraph to family of the passengers. At eight that night, they headed out, equipped with a chart of the island and the surrounding water. But the fog was thick again, and the chart was of little use to them.

Janet and the others were assigned tasks. The ladies were billeted at the superintendent's house and assisted with the meals. As only 12 people could be served at a time, it took most of the day to feed everybody. Others were in charge of drying clothing, gathering firewood, or picking strawberries. Two of the establishment staff and the clergyman passenger carried the drowned women to the cemetery north of the Main Station and buried them there.

By Friday, the castaways were anxious, not knowing whether it would be two weeks or two months before they were rescued. Anger at the loss of life was creating friction. The *State of Virginia* crew refused to accept responsibility, as they said that the accident occurred on a SILE boat, manned by the SILE crew. The SILE crew, stung by the criticism, responded that no lives would have been lost if the boats had been disembarked immediately.

Fleeing the tension of the recriminations, Janet wandered on the beach and watched the children of Sable Island summersault down the dunes, turning turtle over and over until they landed at the bottom in a heap of legs, flying skirts, and bare feet.

On Saturday, the group watched the *Glendon* steam towards Sable Island. Janet and the others gathered their belongings, wet and salt stained as they were, and made their way down to the beach for transfer to the government steamer. By 8 p.m., everybody was on board except Mrs. Widestrand, whose three-year-old son had not yet washed up on shore. She refused to leave Sable until Mrs. McDonald, the wife of the superintendent, promised her that if he did wash up, she would bury him and place flowers on his grave. Finally, after seven days on Sable Island, the castaways left for Halifax.

On July 24, 1879, Janet again set sail for Europe, this time on the steamer *Hibernian*. She thought again of the lighthouse she had seen through the fog, and of how grateful she had been that the lighthouse keeper had heard the cannon. But Janet had no real appreciation for just how arduous the job of lighthouse keeper really was.

Chapter 13
The Lighthouse Keeper: William Merson

I n 1874, William Merson left Sable Island, after serving six years on the lifesaving crew, and headed to Halifax. He was gone for six months. When he returned on March 31, 1875, he brought a wife with him. They'd had a dreadful journey, stuck in the ice at Whitehead for 12 days before crossing to Sable Island. But, Merson thought, Lydia had stood up well and had not complained of the discomfort. She would make a good wife for him in his new job as keeper of the West Light.

Merson was excited, and a little daunted, by the task. The lighthouse was not just a job: his home would also be a refuge for castaways. The isolation of the lighthouse meant that he and Lydia would have little contact with others, except during the brief, daily visits of the beach patrol.

The other 23 hours of each day would be spent maintaining the light, polishing the lens, keeping the buildings in sound repair, and looking after the livestock.

There was no backup staff. Merson was on duty 24 hours a day, 7 days a week, 12 months of the year. The first lighthouse keeper had resigned after a little over 6 months' duty, with no time off. His assistant had withdrawn his resignation on condition that he be transferred from the West Light to the East Light. But as lighthouse keeper, Merson would have his own home, rather than having to live in crew quarters, and for the newlywed, that made the job worthwhile.

He had helped build the lighthouses in 1873. The structures had cost $80,000 — a huge sum considering that the annual budget allotted to the management of Sable Island was only $13,000. The West Light was a handsome thing, Merson thought. Unlike the East Light, which was brown and white, this one was stark white, octagonal, 96 feet tall, and had a revolving white light that gave three flashes at 30-second intervals and then ceased for 90 seconds. The building had slanted walls that made it stronger and provided a wider reflective surface area, making the light seem much larger than it really was. The lighthouse also featured a gallery around the exterior, so that the keeper could clean and repair the glass. Guide wires went from the railing to the roof to deflect the gulls and other birds that were so attracted to the lights. Some mornings, despite this precaution, Merson had to pick up a dozen stunned or dead birds.

Merson proudly escorted Lydia around her new home.

He told her of the lanterns that weighed three tons each and had to be kept in perfect working order. He took her up the stairs, opened the trap door into the lantern, and showed her how the lens floated in a trough of mercury. It was his job, he said, to make sure that the lens was always stable. The mercury expanded or contracted with the temperature, and sometimes, he would have to drain off mercury, or add it. The mercury served another purpose. On those dreadful stormy days, when the wind blew at gale force, the lighthouse would shudder and sway, and the trap door would seem to take on a life of its own as gusts of wind made their way up the stairs. If the lens wasn't floating in its vat of mercury, it wouldn't stay steady, and would break or be damaged. But Merson didn't tell Lydia that yet. There would be plenty of time to teach her the workings of the lighthouse.

He showed her the cover that they draped over the lens in the daytime when the flame was extinguished. Otherwise, the refraction of the sun on the glass could cause a fire, he told her. Merson showed her the belt of wick that was lit by the specially designed burner, and then he took her back down the winding stairs and showed her the gear and heavy weights in the room beneath the lantern. Every four hours those gears had to be wound to keep the light revolving. It took 500 rotations to wind them up, he said. Last, he took her outside and showed her the containers of vegetable oil that fuelled the lamp. They were kept away from the lighthouse in case of fire. The previous lighthouse keeper had had a fire in the steam fog whistle, and if the oil

The light keeper's house, East Light, 1990. When storms
filled the ground floor with sand, the light keeper and his family
moved into the upper storey, until it too was taken over by sand.

had been close, they would have lost the lighthouse and its buildings.

Merson told his wife that when he was called out to a shipwreck, it would be up to her to manage the light until he returned. What neither of them had anticipated was that the lighthouse itself would come into danger.

The winter of 1881 was dreadful. For weeks, the wind and sea assaulted the island until large areas of the west end simply disappeared or were transformed. A single storm destroyed an area 21 metres by 402 metres, then a month later, a nine-metre-wide strip off the west end of the island washed away in a matter of hours. On one particular night, Merson felt the lighthouse sway and shudder from the force of the wind. He went up the stairs to check on the lamp. So strong was the sway up there that the mercury splashed out of the trough. If he put more in, it would simply splash out again, but he would need to keep a watch on it during the night. He checked the door to the gallery and was glad he didn't have to go out there tonight. With its floors sloped away from the building, it would be treacherous. Still, if the windows iced up any more, he might have to risk it. A night like this was a night for shipwrecks, and keeping the light visible might make the difference between a ship avoiding Sable or running aground on its shores.

After the storm, Merson and Lydia saw that the foundation was so eroded that the lighthouse was in danger of falling. The SILE crew dismantled the light and superstructure and moved it east, erecting pole lights on a ship's mast to serve as the light until the technicians came from Montreal to set up the new lantern. While they were building at the new location, a storm swept the old foundation into the ocean. Merson didn't like to think of what would have happened if he and his family had still been living at the old lighthouse site. He and Lydia had several children by then. It was for them that he worried. What happened next would not reassure him.

In 1882, a ferocious storm struck Sable. In the unusually

high tides, an embankment within 12 metres of the Mersons' barn disappeared. Lydia and Merson moved their cows from the barn to the light keeper's porch, but they were no longer confident that this would be enough.

The waves crashed closer and closer. As Merson and his wife and children watched, another 15-metre-wide strip of the island washed away. It was as if a cable simply sliced through the sand and dragged it out into the water. The other men of the SILE came to help, and Lydia took the children to the Main Station for safety. Merson climbed the lighthouse stairs to check the wick and the mercury, and then quickly ran down again. Thank goodness he had to crank the gear mechanism from the bottom. He was getting claustrophobic in the lantern, with the sea encroaching as it was.

Sometime during the night, the barn collapsed and was swept away by the waves. Slightly less than four metres separated the light keeper's porch, with its farm animals, from the sea. The weather calmed, but Merson was not reassured. He packed the family belongings and herded the cows to the paddock at the Main Station.

Merson then returned to the lighthouse to wind the gears. In his short absence, the heavy groundswell from the southeast had undercut the embankment on which the new lighthouse was built, and he saw that the lighthouse now listed to the left. Within an hour, it collapsed, its base literally eaten away from under it.

Lydia was grateful for the respite from the maintenance involved with the light, but by 1883, they were settled in their new house, located farther east on a grassy knoll. She still found it difficult to sleep when the storms raged, and she often got out of bed to check that the water wasn't encroaching on their new place. But in 1884, a fresh tragedy would replace the horrors of the past.

The night of December 19, 1884, was bitterly cold, and a northwest gale brought sleet. Inside the lighthouse, all was well — the light was revolving, as it should. Merson had wound the gears and had settled for his four hours of sleep before he needed to wind them again. Lydia had stayed up late to finish some final preparations for Christmas. She could hear the seals that often came close to the lighthouse during storms, as if they were comforted by its light or size. But the noise changed, and then, at 11:40 p.m., Lydia heard knocking.

She opened the door to find a man on their step. One foot was bare, his clothes were frozen stiff on him, and his hair was in icicles. Lydia yelled for Merson, and together they carried the man, Thomas Huet, inside and wrapped him in warm blankets. They gave him the only medicine they had — a tot of rum. It seemed to revive him, and he mumbled, "Ship, seven." *Good Lord*, thought Merson, *are there six more men out there in these conditions?*

Lydia comforted the man as best she could, while Merson set out for the Main Station. There was no phone at the West Light, no way of communicating with anyone other than by going to their home. Merson would be gone for hours. Lydia would have to care for the castaway, make sure

The East Light (fall 1939) was once the childhood home of Captain James Farquahar, who rose from cabin boy to shipping magnate.

that the children were safe, and manage the lamp. She had two hours before she would have to wind up the gears, and she set to making the man as comfortable as she could. She hoped that the mercury levels would not need adjusting.

It took Merson nearly two hours to walk to Superintendent Robert Boutilier's house. The pair called in three men to assist with the search, and the group set out for the island's west end. Boutilier heard a dog barking, but saw that it was his own Newfoundland and ordered it home. The dog hesitated, so Boutilier yelled at it again.

The men eventually came across the brigantine *A.S.H.*, smashed to pieces on the north shore three miles (4.8 km) west of the Main Station, but there was no sign of her crew. They crisscrossed the beach and the dunes for hours, looking for survivors, their visibility diminished by the wind-driven snow and sand. Despite their efforts, they found no one. After sending the others back to the Main Station for food and rest, Boutilier and Merson headed for the West Light.

At dawn, they set out again. Merson found the first body — that of the second mate, a man named Baptiste — frozen into the ice by the shore of Lake Wallace. Baptiste had managed to crawl only a short distance before the cold had overcome him. Merson left him there and continued his search for survivors. They would come back to retrieve the body later.

Superintendent Boutilier found the next victim, lying in a sheltered hollow. Certain he saw the man move, Boutilier rushed forward, then stopped, aghast. What he'd thought was the movement of a man was instead that of a dog — a large, black Newfoundland so much like his own. The dog lay beside the dead man, its head resting on his chest. Boutilier realized that had he followed the dog the previous night instead of ordering it home, he might have found the man in time, might have saved his life.

Boutilier found himself unable to leave the man, this Captain Lemarchand, as his papers said. His regret was profound, and was to haunt him the rest of his time on Sable Island. For the moment, however, Boutilier could only stroke the dog's head, trying to comfort it.

The SILE crew found a third corpse, that of a sailor

called Noblance, eight miles (12.9 km) east of the wreck. The bodies of two other sailors and an apprentice boy were never found.

The men brought a wagon from the station. They chopped the ice away from the body of Baptiste, loaded it and the two other bodies onto the wagon, took them to the cemetery, and buried them next to the two women from the *State of Virginia* and young Master Widestrand, who had eventually washed up onto the beach.

The captain's dog followed them, and when its master was buried, it lay down beside the grave. It would not leave, no matter how much they coaxed it. For weeks, Merson and the men brought it food. But one day, the dog refused the food, as it did the next day and the one after that. A week later, the dog was dead.

The French government awarded a gold medal to Boutilier and a silver medal to Merson for their efforts in rescuing the crew. But Boutilier, knowing too well that only one man had survived, channelled his energy toward improving the chances of future shipwrecked persons.

Chapter 14
The Pigeon Fancier: Robert Jarvis Boutilier

Following the tragic death of Captain Lemarchand and his men, Superintendent Boutilier changed the patrol system. First, he increased the number of residential stations on the island to six, located three to eight kilometres apart. Then he instituted a ticketing system. A rider from the West End Station would now start eastward on his patrol until he got to the next station. There, he would get his ticket initialled before heading on to the next house, until the entire north beach had been inspected and he had six initials on his ticket. A rider from the East End Station would do the same, travelling the south beach. In such a way, the entire island was covered every day. On stormy or foggy days, when wrecks were most likely, the circuit would be completed twice. If the patrol noticed anything unusual, Boutilier insisted they contact the Main Station immediately.

With the patrols improved, Boutilier next set about improving communication. Since 1884, a telephone had connected the superintendent's house with a few of the other buildings, but the island still lacked a means of contacting the mainland in an emergency. They could send messages with the fishermen, but it might be weeks before they were received in Halifax. Janet Carnochan had suggested an underwater cable in 1879, but the government had rejected the idea. So Boutilier was left to come up with his own solution, and an innovative one at that. Luckily, he had some powerful and influential allies.

The first of these allies was Major-General Donald Roderick Cameron. In 1890, Cameron was commandant at the Royal Military College in Kingston, Ontario. Before that, he had been a Royal Engineer on the Coast Guard and had patrolled the area around Sable Island. He knew Boutilier and his concern for rapid communication, so it was natural that he would choose the isolated Sable Island as a testing ground for his National Messenger Pigeon Service. Cameron believed that carrier pigeons could ensure a reliable, cheap, and swift means of communicating over long distances. His brother-in-law, Sir Charles Hibbert Tupper, was minister of Marine and Fisheries, and approved the plan. Further support came from his father-in-law, the elder Sir Charles Tupper, then living in England. Tupper Sr. told Cameron that the Rothschilds had made a fortune on government bonds because their homing pigeons delivered news of the Battle of Waterloo days before the government messengers arrived in London. He offered to purchase some top-notch English carrier pigeons for the project.

Boutilier knew that the distance to Halifax from Sable Island was well within the range of a good carrier pigeon. They had completed journeys of 644 to 805 kilometres, many times the distance he needed them to travel. Eager to improve communication lines any way he could, the superintendent offered to play a part in the experiment.

Before the Department of Marine and Fisheries purchased any pigeons, it needed housing for them. However, it soon became apparent that no one in the department knew anything about carrier pigeons or their housing requirements, so they hired a naturalist named Andrew Downs and paid him a salary that was equal to 50 percent of Boutilier's salary. Cameron sent detailed blueprints, and the department built the pigeon loft at the marine wharf at Dartmouth.

Sir Charles Tupper had, in the meantime, found a carrier pigeon racing group in Liverpool, England, and had purchased 24 pedigreed and proven racing birds from them. Then, the Count de Bury of Saint John donated six prize-winning Belgian carrier pigeons to the effort. The project was off and running.

Of course, it met with setbacks. Predators killed some of the pigeons during training runs. Other birds simply failed to return. The Department of Marine and Fisheries called in Major Cameron to investigate. He found that though the birds were well cared for, there were problems with the

Land drill, at the Main Station boat house, circa 1898.

record keeping and training. Cameron transferred the care of the carrier pigeon flock to the Royal Engineers, under the direction of Sergeant Uriah Mulholland, the director of signals. Mulholland immediately moved the pigeon loft to Citadel Hill and started serious training.

On February 11, 1893, Mulholland tested his birds. He released a pigeon, recording the time of release and the time of return. The result was disappointing, but it was still early in the project. He took the pigeons farther afield each time. On June 30, 1893, he released 11 pigeons, 40 kilometres from Halifax. Though only four returned, Mulholland had faith in his flock. For the next test, he took the carrier pigeons on the

The Main Station, headquarters of the Sable
Island Lifesaving Establishment, 1899.

government steamer *Newfield*. When they were 145 kilometres from shore, he released them. Unfortunately, he hadn't considered the seagulls, which so pestered the pigeons that they stayed close to the ship, some even making the return trip on the rigging.

After consulting with Boutilier, Mulholland decided to take the pigeons to Sable Island and release them there. But "the birds acted very badly and hung around the island for hours," reported Mulholland. He took them back to Halifax for further training.

On November 23, 1893, Mulholland returned to Sable Island with seven of his best carrier pigeons and handed them over to Superintendent Boutilier. He instructed Boutilier on their care and feeding, and set forth the plan for the next test. Then he boarded the steamer back to Halifax. As agreed, Boutilier waited five days before releasing all seven birds. He hoped that the pigeons would at last prove a reliable means of contacting the mainland in an emergency.

Two reached Halifax, one on November 29 and one on the 30th. The results were not as good as he'd hoped, but the pigeons were certainly as fast as the government steamer. More important, they could be sent when needed. Boutilier felt that the experiment might yet prove to be worthwhile.

In early January 1894, Mulholland shipped his two prize pupils, Carrier Pigeons #113 and #119, back to Sable Island. Less than a week later, on January 12, wreckage washed up onto the beach. A body followed, and then another. Then the sea trunk of Captain Edward Bibber of the Massachusetts schooner *Robert J. Edwards* came ashore. Boutilier now had an assignment for his pigeons. They would take the notification to the mainland of a ship lost with no survivors. But the storm that had destroyed the ship continued, and it was nine days before the weather had calmed enough for the two pigeons to take off with any chance of success.

On January 21, 1894, Boutilier wrote the same message on linen papers, placed them inside two tubes, and attached one to each pigeon's leg. He waited until 10 a.m. to release them, and then watched as they headed due north. A good sign, thought Boutilier, who had rather feared they might make right for the barn by the Main Station.

The old Main Station, 1974. The storms that blast Sable Island wreak havoc on buildings as well as ships.

Pigeon #113 was never seen again. Pigeon #119 had started off heading north, but then it had either veered or was blown off course, so that at 4 p.m. it landed on the deck of the fishing schooner *Mabel B. Leighton*, 200 miles (321.9 km) west–southwest of Sable Island. The crew picked up the pigeon, removed the message from its leg, and tried to revive the clearly exhausted bird. After a time, they released it. To their dismay, it flew a short distance and then plummeted into the ocean and drowned.

The captain of the *Mabel B. Leighton* had understood the message the pigeon had been carrying, but he had three more weeks of fishing and didn't return to port until February 11. Though the message had been delayed, Boutilier was nevertheless impressed with the distance the pigeon had flown, and they continued with the experiments.

That summer, the Royal Engineers sent 33 pigeons to Sable Island. Boutilier released them all, but only seven reached Halifax. On the next trial, six of the seven birds successfully returned to their loft. Boutilier was encouraged. Sable Island still had its share of wrecks, but there were other pressing needs for contact.

In August of that year, Mrs. Boutilier died after a short illness. There had been no time to get a doctor, not even an opportunity to inform anyone of her illness. That same month, a plague of locusts destroyed the island's vegetable crop and brought the livestock and Sable Island horses close to starvation after devouring both the hay and the marram grass on which the horses depended. Boutilier knew he would be short of provisions, but he had no way of informing Halifax to bring extra supplies on their next run.

Although Boutilier hadn't given up on the pigeons, the Department of Marine and Fisheries terminated the National Carrier Pigeon Service and established a wireless service between Halifax and Sable Island. The new system, though heralded as both "practical and reliable," would not be without its own problems.

Chapter 15
The Brass-Pounder: Thomas Raddall

Thomas Raddall was 17 years old when he was assigned to the Sable Island wireless station in April 1921. He felt as if he'd been sentenced to Siberia, but he nevertheless knew that he had to accept the posting. If he turned down Sable, he would be given another fishing trawler. His age made him ineligible for his first-class wireless ticket, and until he had that ticket, he went wherever the Marconi Company sent him.

Raddall could work at 20 words (100 letters) a minute, and had a "hand" that was recognized up and down the coast. He knew that many still considered the telegraph a fad, even black magic, but after the loss of the *Titanic*, all ships were ordered to install wireless. Still, Raddall and the other wireless operators were considered oddities, men who spoke in dots and dashes and gazed off into the distance as if in a trance, listening for what was indecipherable to others. Teased for playing with knobs and sparks while "real men" fished, he was given the nickname "Sparks." But Raddall preferred the term "brass-pounder." That's what the wireless operators called themselves — it described the way they had to work the heavy brass key.

Sable Island did have one attraction for Raddall. Next to Cape Race, Newfoundland, it was the busiest and most important station on Canada's east coast, handling communication with all the liners crossing to Europe. As one of the initial wireless stations, it had sent its first official message on June 27, 1905, and was said to have heard the distress call from the *Titanic* on April 15, 1912. Lately, the station had grown very busy, serving as a relay station between fishing trawlers and the mainland. Raddall would be challenged in this post, perhaps would even become famous because of it. There was a cachet to being a brass-pounder at Sable Island. And he knew that he only had to commit to one year.

Raddall had heard about the mutiny in 1919, when the wireless operators had burned the wireless station to the ground to protest working conditions. The men had denied the arson, but witnesses had seen them hurling gasoline onto the structure. All but one of the men had been fired, but since then, every wireless operator was granted a shore furlough after one year. Following that, they could return to Sable or were free to go. Raddall planned to leave.

On April 21, 1921, Raddall packed his sea chest and made his way to the Department of Marine and Fisheries dock, where the pigeon loft had once been. There, he boarded the government ship *Dollard* and had his first shock of many. Raddall had spent two years on trawlers and was used to the crew bunks on those ships. But on the *Dollard*, he was shown to a lavish cabin furnished with red carpet, a green plush couch, maple panelling, a mahogany berth with brass handles, and an adjoining bathroom. He had heard that the brass-pounders received better wages and better provisions since the mutiny, and if this cabin was any indication of the quarters he would have on the island, then things were looking up, he thought. But he learned that the cabin had been furnished for the department deputy minister, who had yet to sail on the ship.

When they reached Sable Island, they anchored a mile (1.6 km) off the north shore and transferred to the surfboats. Everybody on the island was gathered on the beach — some 44 men, women, and children. Raddall thought they had come to welcome him, but it was the supply ship they greeted with such excitement. He looked around and saw an expanse of sand and water, where nothing grew higher than his knees. Marram grass covered much of the dunes, but still the "sand moved with the wind like drifts of snow," he later wrote. He thought it a desolate place, a "hell-on-earth."

It seemed to Raddall that the establishment probably hadn't grown much since James Morris's time. He could see the Main Station, the West Light, the superintendent's house, the lifeboat crew barracks, and the Sailors' Home. All were within a mile (1.6 km) of each other near the west end of

Lake Wallace. He saw the wooden watchtower, topped with a crows-nest to watch for ships. Raddall couldn't imagine being up there when the winds blew.

He hadn't located the wireless station yet, although he could see the topmost section of a radio mast projecting above a dune. Raddall hoisted his shabby trunk onto his shoulder and set off. He saw the people watching him expectantly, and he soon knew why.

Away from the hard-packed beach, the sand was deep — so deep that he sank mid-calf with every step. He glanced at the people, acknowledged their knowing looks, and sensed there was much more he would learn in the months ahead. He now understood why the wheels on the wagon were so wide. He set out again, moving very slowly, but eager to see where he would be living for the next 12 months.

The wireless station was a white clapboard bungalow, newly constructed to replace the building that had burned down. Raddall entered the narrow hallway. On his left he could see the wireless room. It had a long table that ran the full length of the room under the only window. Sitting at the table was one of his co-workers, listening intently to the sound of the dit-dit-dit da-dit-da. The man glanced up at Raddall, gave him a welcoming nod, and then concentrated on his work again. Raddall knew he looked just like this man when he was working; he had that same tension to his body, as if he were trying to see the message he was hearing. Set up on the table was the apparatus of his trade — two varnished wooden boxes faced with ebonite and studded with knobs and dials, and a message slip and pencil. On the right lay the transmitting key, with its thick brass shank and round black knob. On the wall to his left, a black switchboard with switches, voltmeters, and ammeters. Clips of message forms hung from the wainscoting.

Raddall was relieved to see a small iron stove in the corner of the room. At least he would be warm when he worked. He'd heard that it could get very cold here, that an inkwell in one of the bedrooms had once stayed frozen for three months. His own room was next to the wireless room. It was tiny, with a small twin bed and a battered chest of drawers. But after the crew quarters on ship, it was roomy enough. And best of all, it was his own. He set his chest down and went on to look at the rest of the quarters. His co-worker's room was next to his. At the end of the hall were the married quarters, where the chief wireless operator and his wife lived, and then there was a room for the cook, a bathroom, and finally the engine room, which reeked of hot oil.

Like all the wireless operators, Raddall had been fully trained in maintaining the equipment and could install and repair everything from the keys to the aerials. But he knew he would have his work cut out for him trying to maintain this beast of an engine. While he watched, it let out a sound like a rifle shot and set into motion the two flywheels that powered the belts. The revolving brass studs on the generator shaft gave off flashes, accompanied by a sound like a trumpet. Raddall felt perfectly at home looking at this monstrosity. As deafening as it was after the silence at sea, he was used to it. After a day or two it wouldn't even wake him up, though his room was across the hall. There was a muffling drum that fit over the spark disc to dampen the noise, but Raddall knew he wouldn't use it. It was too much bother to take it off every time he needed to clean and adjust the studs.

Raddall loved the work of the wireless operator. He could sit at his desk and, simply by putting on those great uncomfortable metal headphones and slipping his hand onto a key, enter an entirely different world. Within seconds, he could be on a fishing trawler on the Grand Banks, a passenger cruise ship in the North Atlantic, or a tramp steamer with a cargo of iron bound for France or Spain.

He especially loved the emergencies, which were heralded by the three dots, three dashes, and three dots all strung together. Then, the chatter of all the other wireless stations from Labrador to Florida would stop. Raddall, at his listening post would strain to hear the voice of the ship in distress, his finger almost vibrating at the key, anticipating his response. The message would be relayed, and Raddall would write it down on a square of paper with his short pencil. He would check the charts on the wall to pinpoint the location of the ship. Then he would send out a message asking for nearby ships to respond. In these instances, Raddall could imagine the interior of the ship, feel the heat of a fire in the galley, and smell the sweat of the crew working at breakneck speed to repair a rudder chain. He could taste the sour bile of fear.

That's what made it so odd that when a ship sunk at Sable Island a month after he arrived, he was totally oblivious to the event.

The American schooner *Esperanto* won the inaugural International Fisherman's Schooner Race in 1920. On May 30, 1921, she struck the sunken remains of the *State of Virginia* and sunk.

That ship was the schooner *Esperanto*, winner of the inaugural International Fisherman's Schooner Race, held the previous October in Halifax. The race had been a fabulous affair, a celebration of the rivalry between the fishermen of Lunenburg, Nova Scotia, and Gloucester, Massachusetts. In the "best two out of three races," the American *Esperanto* had beaten the Canadian *Delawana* and had taken home the $4000 first prize and the silver cup. She was a beautiful ship, with sleek lines, and she was capable of amazing speed when going windward. But she was also a working fishing schooner, and after the glory of her victory, she returned to fishing the waters off Sable Island.

Her captain, Tom Benham, knew the best catches were close to the south shore where the waters were warmest, and on May 30, 1921, the *Esperanto* and another schooner, the *Elsie II*, were anchored half a mile (0.8 km) off the south beach. Raddall, walking on the beach before his four o'clock shift, could see the dory men catching cod with hand lines.

When dusk came, rather than sail around the northwest bar to anchor on the safer north side, Benham manoeuvred the *Esperanto* toward the gap in the bar. He never made it that far. The fully loaded schooner struck the sunken remains of the *State of Virginia*, which had been wrecked 42 years earlier. The *Esperanto*'s hull was torn open and she filled with water and sank.

In the morning, the Sable Island patrol reported a pair of topmasts sticking up out of the sea off the south beach. The lifeboat crew rowed out and found a schooner "sunk with all sail set and all her dories nested on her deck." They took a boathook and managed to loosen the topmost dory. On the gunwale was the word *Esperanto*. With a heavy heart, Raddall sent a message to Halifax reporting that the *Esperanto* had sunk and that the crew was presumed drowned. But amazingly, the next day, the Halifax Marconi office notified Sable Island that the schooner *Elsie II* had rescued the entire crew of the *Esperanto* and transported them safely to Halifax. Lacking wireless, the fishing schooner had been unable to notify the SILE until they reached the mainland.

Before the *Esperanto* was smashed to pieces by the waves, Raddall was able to salvage a piece of canvas from one of her sails, which he painted and made into a floor covering for the wireless office. The SILE crew repaired one of the schooner's dories for use by the establishment. But five years later, there would be a storm of such magnitude that not even that much would remain of the ships caught in its fury.

Chapter 16
The Highliner:
The *Sylvia Mosher*

J ohn Mosher of Lunenburg, Nova Scotia, was a skipper at 20. By age 25, he was captain of the 78-ton fishing schooner *Sylvia Mosher*. She was a very fine fishing vessel, measuring 118.6 feet in length and 27 feet across the beam, and having a 10-foot-deep hold. Built by John McLean and Sons of Mahone Bay, Nova Scotia, she started life in 1925 with some excitement. Mosher's young wife, Florence, had christened the ship, naming her after their infant daughter. Then, as the ship slid down the launching ramp, the *Sylvia Mosher* tipped, hanging suspended by the guide ropes for what seemed like an eternity, until the shipyard workers had been able to right her without damaging her sleek lines.

The *Sylvia Mosher* had an excellent first season and was named "highliner" for the biggest catch in the fleet. In the spring of her second year, she again brought in the biggest catch. Some said it was because of Mosher's skill. He would bring her in close to the shoals where the fish were so numerous — closer than others dared. He seemed to fear nothing.

Mosher needed to have a good season, for he was having a new house built for his family. He owned 5 of the 64 shares in the *Sylvia Mosher*. The previous year, she had brought in 624,592 pounds of fish and had paid $189 a share. At this rate, she would soon pay off her purchase price of $2496. And because she was "highliner" and he a well-respected captain, she attracted the best crew. That always translated into camaraderie aboard ship, and a big catch.

On July 12, 1926, the *Sylvia Mosher* set sail for the Sable Island Bank. On the morning of Saturday, August 7, she was one of a dozen fishing boats anchored off the south shore of the island, her holds close to full of wet salted cod. Mosher and the captain of the *Sadie Knickle* liked to fish "right in against the bar down near the middle station," and were less than half a mile (0.8 km) offshore, close to where the *Esperanto* and the *State of Virginia* had wrecked. The weather was calm and the fog was dense, as it so often was in the summer.

At 4 a.m., the men of the *Sylvia Mosher* got up, ate their breakfast, and dressed in their woollen trousers and chequered work shirts. They lowered the dories, loaded their gear, and set off from the schooner. The crew was looking forward to the next day, for they never worked on the Sabbath. The captain often invited the SILE's superintendent onto the ship for lunch, and then the men would follow him back to the island. They would play in the shallow water or go exploring on the beach, looking at the stuff that had come off wrecks. Some days they chased the horses, sneaking up on them and making a dreadful racket so that they went off across the sand, bucking and running so fast the men had no chance of catching them. But that Saturday, the weather was shifty. There was hardly a ripple at first, and then short bursts of wind — cat's-paws that swirled the water's surface.

Cat's-paws usually heralded a storm, and at 2 p.m., crewmembers of the *Sylvia Mosher* fired off the swivel (a small cannon), signalling everyone to come back on board. The fishermen immediately hauled in their lines and returned to the schooner. They dressed the catch and prepared for the gale they knew was inevitable.

First, they put any loose gear in the hold and battened down the hatches with canvas and a bar. Then they reefed the foresail and set a riding sail aft. The wind rose to 129 kilometres per hour from the southeast, threatening to tear the sails to shreds. Next the rain came, torrents of water that blinded the men as effectively as the fog. They hung bags of cod oil over the side of the ship in an attempt to calm the seas, but these seas would not be calmed. The harvest of fish in the hold served as additional ballast, but the waves were now breaking over the deck. Any gear not lashed down was swept away.

There were 24 men on the *Sylvia Mosher*. Included were multiple members of the same family: Captain Mosher and his brother Aubrey; three brothers of the Whynacht family — William, Ladonia, and Kenneth, together with Kenneth's son, Don; Caleb and Guy Baker and Caleb's son, Carman; and brothers John and Warren Wagner. Thirteen members of the crew were married, and many had young children.

When the storm continued to rise, some of the men went below, sealing the companionway behind them and laying in their bunks waiting for deliverance or death. Others climbed high into the rigging, seeking to get above the reach of the waves and wanting to meet their fate head on.

The winds churned up the water. No longer were there peaks and vales to the waves, but a seething boiling mass that attacked from all sides, without any rhythm. Because the *Sylvia Mosher* was in relatively shallow water, the seas broke from the bottom and the schooner was tossed up, crashed down, hurled to one side, and then tipped to the other. Each wave brought sand into the boat, sand that choked the men on deck and, coupled with the salt water, made their eyes sting.

The storm continued through the night. On Sunday morning, the patrols went out and rode the beaches. They saw no evidence of wrecked vessels and marvelled that the *Sylvia Mosher* and *Sadie Knickle* had both managed to haul anchor and sail away from the treacherous bar in time. That evening, the men patrolled again and reported to Superintendent Henry that the fishing schooners seemed to have come through the storm unscathed. On Monday, August 9, the report was the same, and the men of the SILE breathed a sigh of relief.

But Tuesday, August 10, brought a different emotion. The morning patrol reported that six empty dories from the *Sylvia Mosher* had washed ashore on the north beach. Had the *Sylvia Mosher* crossed the bar, or had she sunk on the south side and her dories been carried by the current to the north side? The SILE crew took a closer look at the northeast and northwest bars. That was when they saw the outline of a vessel. Henry sent a message to the minister of Marine and Fisheries: "Lunenburg schooner *Sylvia Mosher* total wreck on outer bar, north side, near #4 station, lying on side. No sign of crew."

The SILE crew knew the *Sylvia Mosher* had 20 dories. She was a new, well-built fishing vessel, not like some of the other ships that had wrecked on Sable Island. Perhaps her crew had had time to get into their dories and were now on the open water heading for Canso. They would only need eight or nine dories, and 14 were not yet accounted for.

There were no bodies, but the waters around Sable Island seldom gave up their dead. The currents and waves saw to that, as did the sharks. Still, there was reason to hope. The men knew the story of Richard Clarke, knew that he had been wrecked in an August Gale and had made it all the way to Newfoundland with one dory and a single oar. They telegraphed Halifax and requested that the government steamer *Lady Laurier* be dispatched to look for survivors.

On Wednesday, August 11, the schooner *Mary Ruth* hobbled into Lunenburg Harbour. She had been fishing near Sable Island and would have ridden out the same storm. The hopes of the community went up, but when they saw the state of the ship, what little hope they had was shattered. The *Mary Ruth* looked as if a bomb had exploded on her deck. Her sails were torn, but more significant, her dories had been swept into the water by the surf, a surf that had broken the cook stove and injured nine of the crew, fracturing bones, bruising skin, and cutting flesh.

The *Lady Laurier* searched for three days and then returned with news of wreckage strewn about, but no sign of survivors. Later that evening, the Sable Island wireless operator reported that two more dories had drifted ashore.

On August 16, 1926, the Honourable W. A. Black requested that a seaplane from Eastern Passage Air Station fly over the area in hopes of finding some trace of survivors. On the 17th, he was told there was no plane available. Black pursued his request and discovered that not only was there a plane, but that it sat ready on the airfield, its tank full of gas. When he asked why it couldn't be used, he was told that there was no flying officer at the airfield. Black countered by locating an experienced pilot at McNab's Island. Then he was told that the air station could not approve the flight, that approval would have to come from Ottawa. Black sent a telegraph to the Department of Defence requesting urgent approval of his petition. He never received a response.

More dories washed up on Sable Island, but so damaged were they that it was impossible to tell which ship they had come from. It was becoming obvious that there was more than one ship's wreckage coming ashore, and it was soon confirmed that the *Sadie Knickle* and her crew of 23 were also lost.

No plane ever searched the water for the 47 missing crewmembers of the *Sylvia Mosher* and *Sadie Knickle*. It would be 15 years before an aerial search for survivors was conducted near Sable Island. And when it happened, they were looking not for fishermen, but for a missing plane.

Chapter 17
The Pilot: Flying Officer Lieutenant G. B. Snow

On June 1, 1941, four airmen went missing while protecting a convoy travelling through the waters near Sable Island. There had been no distress call, but the Bristol Bolingbroke Mk IV s/n 9007, piloted by C766 Squadron Leader Richard Brock Wylie of Estevan, Saskatchewan, had failed to return to the RCAF base at Glace Bay, Nova Scotia. There was a chance that it had simply crashed, but there was a real possibility that it had been shot down.

In the years since the wrecking of the *Sylvia Mosher*, the SILE had changed its focus. As more and more ships were motorized, few found themselves helpless in the island's currents and surf. There was new danger in the water now. Sable Island was strategically located on the principal convoy route from Halifax to Iceland and England. German submarines hunted in the waters between Sable Island and Halifax, and between Sable Island and the eastern seaboard. Sometimes, if the surf was quiet, island staff could hear the engines of the enemy subs as they rose to the surface off the island to make repairs. The SILE crew recorded these events, as well as any suspicious activity by foreign vessels, and they manned the weather station.

On June 3, the RCAF sent a Lockheed Hudson bomber from the Bomber Reconnaissance (BR) Unit at RCAF Station Dartmouth to look for the downed Bolingbroke. On board were the pilot, Flying Officer Lieutenant G. B. Snow; his navigator, First Officer I. L. G. Gillis; wireless operators Corporal D. E. Craig and Leading Aircraftman G. A. Dillworth; and medical officer Flight Lieutenant F. J. Bell.

The men searched as best they could, flying a grid, first one way and then another, combing the vast area for any sign of survivors or wreckage. They looked for subs, too, knowing that they were notoriously difficult to spot. The best chance was to surprise a U-boat while it was on the surface or in the process of submerging. The problem was that lookouts on the subs could spot a plane, especially one the size of the Hudson, long before the crew of the plane could spot the submarine. The Hudson's undersurface had recently been painted white, making it less distinguishable than before, especially on foggy days.

The men knew the history of submarine warfare in this part of the Atlantic. On August 2, 1918, submarine

U-156 under the command of Kapitanleutnant Richard Feldt had intercepted the four-masted schooner *Dornfontein* six miles (9.7 km) south of Grand Manan, New Brunswick. The Germans had taken the fishing crew onto the submarine and then looted the vessel and burned it to the waterline.

On July 7 and 8, 1918, the same submarine, hunting in the waters near Sable Island, had sunk the Norwegian ship *Marosa* and the schooner *Manx King*. Then she had gone on to sink five American ships in quick succession before returning to prey on the Canadians.

On August 20, 1918, the trawler *Triumph* had been fishing at Middle Bank, north of Sable Island, when U-156 surfaced and fired a warning shot across her bow. The German submariners had not harmed the crew, but had boarded the *Triumph* and installed a wireless radio, two light artillery guns, and 25 bombs. They had then set the crew adrift in a dory and headed the armed, German-manned fishing trawler straight into the heart of the Nova Scotia fishing fleet.

The *Triumph* was familiar to the fishermen of the bank, and she was able to come within close range before the fishermen were aware of the German ensign. Over the next four days, the Germans sank seven fishing schooners. Each time, they released the crew unharmed and set them adrift in their dories. But the *Triumph* was coal-fired and the manoeuvre had used up her supplies, so the Germans scuttled her.

The crew on board the Hudson knew why they had been taught about the *Triumph*, and they doubled their vigilance, looking not just for their missing plane and for submarines, but for any other traffic on the water. They noted every schooner and trawler, even the supply ship that was taking Superintendent Don Johnson to Halifax for a medical appointment. There had been no sub sinking of Canadian ships in this war so far, but the men knew it was just a matter of time. They knew subs were lurking in the water.

The plane descended lower. The fog was intensifying, making visibility difficult. They'd be lucky to see a whole squadron of planes, let alone a single airplane. The stories they had heard of Sable Island shipwrecks took on new relevance. The men were flying blind, but at least they were in the air. It wasn't like being on a ship where you could run aground or run into another ship.

But Sable Island was a magnet for more than ships. In that entire expanse of ocean, with thousands of kilometres of empty airspace, the low-flying RCAF twin engine Lockheed Hudson Bomber struck the Sable Island wireless mast, shearing off a wing. The plane veered out to sea and plunged into the surf 137 metres off the beach.

The SILE reported in to the Department of Transport. The department, in turn, notified the RCAF headquarters and, on June 4, Air Vice Marshall N. R. Anderson, commanding officer of the Eastern Air Command, issued a press release stating that the navy was continuing its search for the crew of the missing plane. But now, one of those naval ships had another assignment: she would be bringing back the bodies of the five dead airmen.

Superintendent Johnson was in Halifax at the time of the

crash, and he travelled back to Sable Island on the navy vessel. An ex-RCMP officer, Johnson was a capable diver, and when they arrived at Sable Island, he gathered his diving gear from the Main Station and prepared to assist with the recovery of bodies from the downed plane. Then he returned to the wreckage and retrieved the logbooks and any other classified material, to prevent it from falling into the hands of the Germans.

Sable Island, home of more than 345 known shipwrecks, had added a plane wreck to its tally. The Navy Court of Inquiry found that the cause of the crash was "low flying in heavy fog and error in altimeter due to lower atmospheric pressure at Sable Island than at Dartmouth." Among the recommendations was that "weather reports be submitted from Sable Island hourly." The original missing plane was never found, nor was there any clue as to its disappearance.

The Hudson was the first airplane crash at Sable Island, but it would not be the last. On August 20, 1942, a Supermarine Walrus flying boat, affectionately known as the "Shagbat," stationed at the Fleet Air Arm on Sable Island, was forced down on the ocean. For three days it stayed afloat, its crew safe inside, until ships of the convoy HX204 rescued them. Unfortunately, the Shagbat sank while being towed by the corvette HMCS *Napanee.* Then, on February 12, 1945, a Consolidated Liberator Mk GR IV experienced engine problems and touched down on Lake Wallace. The crew escaped unharmed.

Stories of survival at Sable Island are numerous. Perhaps the most amazing of them all is the story of the Sable Island horses.

Chapter 18
The Survivors: The Sable Island Horses

The Sable Island horse galloped on the south beach, his hooves leaving tracks in the damp sand. He was nimble and sure-footed, could sense where the water saturated the beach, creating areas of quicksand. He was here on Sable Island, free and healthy despite attempts to eradicate him, hunt him, profit from him, and eventually to declare him "surplus property." Legend had said he was a survivor of Spanish shipwrecks, but the truth was far less romantic.

Few horses ever survived a shipwreck. Most were too weak after months at sea on poor rations and would have been no match for the surf at Sable Island. Many horses never even made it to a ship's destination. When a ship got into trouble at sea, when it ran short of water or needed to jettison cargo, horses were the first to be sacrificed.

André Le Mercier placed 20 to 30 horses on Sable Island in the 1750s, but they were all eventually removed or killed. Wreckers hunted them for food, and for their hides and hair, which were used in making leather goods, furniture stuffing, and plaster. They sawed off the horses' hooves and shipped them by the barrel to be made into glue. By the time Le Mercier finally gave up on his quest for ownership of the island, few horses remained. Those that were left, he took back to Boston.

In 1755, Thomas Hancock placed 60 horses on the island, horses that he'd obtained from those confiscated from the Acadians. These are the ancestors of the island horses.

The Sable Island horse that turned off the beach and trotted into the dunes was of strong stock and had survived numerous assaults. During the American War of Independence, both British and American ships took horses from the island for remounts. By 1800, cargoes of horses were being stolen and sent to the West Indies for use in the sugar mills and plantations.

Governor Sir John Wentworth was well aware of the value of these horses and ensured that any profit from them made its way into the coffers of the Nova Scotia government, rather than the moneybags of mere criminals. When he sent James Morris to Sable Island in 1801, part of Morris's job was to "carefully preserve and diligently to encourage the growth and increase of all Horses."

Morris tried to capture the horses, but his own mount, Jolly, was unable to keep up with, let alone outrun, these adept island horses. He tried snares, but the horses avoided them. Morris drove them into pens, but the horses galloped through the fencing. He dug a long ramp in the sand that ended in a pit, but the horses galloped down the ramp, turned, and then ran up the slope again.

When Morris finally did succeed in capturing and training a few, he found them sure-footed and of amazing stamina. In 1803, he shipped four to Halifax as a way of testing the market. Sir John Wentworth took one for his son and one for himself. Two others went to city officials. They were well liked, and it became fashionable to have a Sable Island horse for your child.

But the development of the Sable Island Lifesaving Establishment brought an unforeseen danger to the horses. The number of shipwreck survivors and the length of their stay on the island, combined with the inadequate supplies for so many, meant that some of the colts and stallions were culled and used for meat. When the SILE ran short of feed for the hogs, they slaughtered the old mares, for the hogs rejected seal meat.

Superintendent Edward Hodgeson respected the toughness of the Sable Island horses but felt they weren't heavy enough to pull the lifeboat carriers through the sand. Sometimes the horses had to travel 26 kilometres to get to a wreck, and then travel the 26 kilometres back to bring survivors to the Main Station. Hodgeson imported an in-foal draught mare, with plans to crossbreed her with the indigenous horses. But Sable Island is not kind to its imports, and the mare died before the first foal was born. A second pregnant mare aborted during the sea voyage from Halifax. Several "superior" stallions were imported between 1801 and 1830. The Sable Island stallions killed all of them.

Joseph Darby, that fallen hero, tried to retain the best of the stock, but the demand for them seemed insatiable. One year, 300 horses were shipped to the mainland, leaving only 250 behind. In 1853, 52 horses were shipped to Provincetown, Massachusetts, on the schooner *Smith Tuttle*. They were sold as poor quality animals: "5 horses of one year old @ 20 shillings each; 22 horses of 2 years old @ 30 shillings each; 15 full-grown horses and mares @ 60 shillings each; and 10 mares with colts @ 60 shillings each." Such low prices often bought poor homes.

The Sable Island horse that cantered over the marram grass had had a noble competitor once. Superintendent Robert Boutilier had imported Jack of Trumps in July 1885. The stallion had raced in Boston, Bangor, and all over the Maritimes, and he thrived at Sable Island, alone at the west end with his 14 handpicked mares. Boutilier had removed any competition by gelding or shipping all "entires" from the west end, and by August, Trump's mares were all in foal. But then Boutilier made a fatal mistake.

In September, he shipped 50 horses from the east end of the island. The east end stallions travelled west looking for the lost members of their herd. They didn't find them, but they did find Jack of Trumps and his group of 14 mares. The stallions attacked him, broke his shoulder, and drove him

On a chilly spring day, a band of Sable
Island horses walk along the low tide line.

into the quicksand, where Boutilier found him dead. He had
only survived two months on Sable Island.

The Sable Island horse that bucked as he ran, his mane
so long it touched the wild orchids in the valley, no longer
feared the roundups that had injured and killed his ancestors. At one time, they ran the horses into pens, pens they
built more strongly than before. Some of the superintendents
withheld food and water to make the horses docile. Then,
when they were ready to load, they caught each horse with a
looped lasso on the end of a long pole. Drawing the lasso tight,
they throttled the horse to the point of strangulation, until he
could no longer struggle. They flipped him on his side, tied
his four legs together, and heaved him onto a four-handled
stretcher or "pony barrow," which they then put on the surf

boat for the trip to the government supply ship anchored offshore. At the ship, they hoisted the horses aboard in slings and lowered them into the hold. In later years, they lifted them by their feet, maiming and crippling them.

In August 1873, the *Halifax Daily Reporter* reviled the horses: "It is hoped that no more of these horses will be brought to Halifax. Our present breed of horse is in all conscience, low enough without forcing these degenerate animals upon the country." Others applauded the animals. The *Morning Herald* of the same day said, " Eleven ponies just arrived from Sable Island. They are decidedly the best lot ever offered. They are all first class."

There was no guarantee of a good home. Most were sold to fishermen and street vendors. The skewbald and pie-bald horses were bought by butchers and other tradesmen, and for children's mounts. Some made their way along the coast and worked for seaweed and dulse harvesters. Others went to Cape Breton to become pit ponies in the coalmines, their size making it possible to cut narrower and therefore cheaper seams into the rocks. Once they entered the mines, they never saw the light of day again, only the glow of the coal lamps. And because of the steady market for pit ponies, the paint horses and the light-coloured ones were culled before they could breed — mine operators didn't want animals that showed the dirt.

Alexander Graham Bell brought two Sable Island horses home for his children after visiting the island. Other horses found homes pulling doctors' buggies, for their sure-footedness and stamina made them ideal for someone who had to go out in all weather conditions and at any time of the day or night. In 1879, there was a flurry of interest in the Sable Island horses as polo mounts for the officers of Halifax. Over time, more than 5000 Sable Island horses were shipped from their home.

The Sable Island horse that splashed into the shallow water at Lake Wallace was no longer in danger from horse dealers. After World War II, the government took over responsibility for the island and decided to sell the horses en masse. The government had no intention of becoming responsible for the care and feeding of this "surplus stock," and it invited ideas for the eradication of the horses. A sharpshooter volunteered to go on the island and gun the horses down. A farmer suggested developing a fox farm on the island and using the horses as a source of fresh and readily available feed. Both ideas were rejected, and the government authorized the Crown Assets Disposal Corporation to get rid of the animals.

A buyer from Kentville, Nova Scotia, bought 150 of them and headed to Sable Island to collect them. But he had not counted on the difficulty in getting an unwilling and terrified 700-pound animal to cross a mile (1.6 km) of ocean to a schooner. The pony barrows were long gone, so these men rigged up another means of transport. They tied the two front legs together and the hind legs together and lay the horses piggyback over barrels. Then they towed them out to the vessel. Several horses were injured in loading; others were damaged during transport.

On a warm day in June, two Sable Island mares and their month-old foals stand on a dune overlooking the West Ponds.

The Nova Scotia Society for the Prevention of Cruelty to Animals (NSSPCA) heard of the fiasco and met the ship in Halifax. One horse was so badly injured that the NSSPCA agent was forced to shoot him. He threatened charges of cruelty to animals. But it wasn't clear whom he should charge — the horse dealer or the government who had transported the horses. The government resolved the issue by discontinuing its plans to ship the animals.

The battle took on an ecological bent. The government stated that the horses were destroying the ecology of the island, trampling the marram grass that anchored the sand on the dunes. A former Sable Island boatman, now a member of Parliament, argued the opposite: the horses were all that kept the island alive, for they fertilized and conserved the grass. The horses won a reprieve.

But other politicians wrote letters for a succession of reputable horse owners and disreputable horse dealers, authorizing them to take possession of the horses if they could win the approval of the NSSPCA. Mr. M. H. Sarty, secretary manager of the NSSPCA, dug in his heels. Far from giving approval, he insisted that he would lay charges against anyone who tried to forcibly remove the animals. The Sable Island horses had their second reprieve, but, like the first, it would be short-lived.

Ten years later, in 1960, the Canadian government declared that the horses were starving and should be removed from the island. Again, the Crown Assets Disposal Corporation printed a notice offering them for sale — singly or in lots. The battle was played out in the *Halifax Herald* newspapers of May and June 1960.

On May 27, the NSSPCA let fly the opening salvo, publicly opposing the removal of the horses. The Ontario SPCA followed suit, urging an end to the sale and slaughter of the horses. People wrote letters to the editor. They suggested that if the Department of Transport was so keen on having an auction, they should have one, but auction off the minister rather than the horses.

In June, Colonel Sidney C. Oland, a Halifax businessman, farmer, and soldier, recounted his own childhood pleasures with the horses. He and his friends had fought many a battle with their cavalry of Sable Island horses against the infantry of neighbourhood children. He appealed to parents to buy these horses for their children, to prevent the animals ending up in abattoirs, in glue factories, or in the hands of horse dealers.

Horse lovers across Canada took up the cry. They wrote to their members of Parliament, to the newspapers, to their SPCAs, and to Prime Minister Diefenbaker. Schoolchildren sent thousands of letters beseeching the prime minister and the minister of transport to save the Sable Island "ponies." The government caved under the pressure, and the prime minister announced that the 250 Sable Island horses would be allowed to remain on the island.

The battle seemed won. But then, George Ellison Noble, lighthouse keeper at Sable Island from 1953 to 1956, contacted the Halifax newspapers. He was appalled at the decision. He said that in his three years on Sable Island, he had seen more than 250 horses die of colic and starvation.

This was the opening the horse dealers were looking for. They suggested that the government might as well slaughter the horses as have them starve. Hugh Stewart, an Ontario farmer, petitioned the navy for help in removing the horses from the island. He said that he had visited Sable Island in 1958–1959, and that the horses had been in dreadful condition — malnourished and weak. The government had been so concerned that it had dropped five tons of hay to help stave off starvation. It seemed that perhaps the government's decision to remove the horses had not been simply a cost-cutting measure.

But more letters poured in from Canada, Britain, and Europe in favour of leaving the horses in their natural habitat, and in 1961, the government passed the Sable Island regulations: "No person should, without prior written permission from the District Marine Agent of the Department of Transport at Dartmouth, Nova Scotia, molest, interfere with, feed or otherwise have anything to do with the ponies of Sable Island." The fine for doing so was $200 or two weeks in jail, or both.

The Sable Island horse racing down to the waterline would, for better or worse, remain on the island to live, or die as nature dictated.

Epilogue

The last Sable Island superintendent, Arthur Dooks, left in 1960, and only the weather station remained staffed on a permanent basis. The Main Station, Sailors' Home, and East and West light keepers homes have all fallen in ruins or lie buried beneath the sand.

In the spring of 1995, the federal government announced plans to abandon Sable Island by April 1997. In fear that this unique and very vulnerable environment would be overrun and destroyed by those who didn't recognize its scientific, ecological, and historical value, Nova Scotians campaigned for long-term conservation of this island that is so dear to them.

On January 31, 2005, in response to their efforts, the government of Canada announced that it would ensure that Sable Island would "be preserved and protected for generations to come," and that the best way to do this would be to maintain a human presence on the island. The Department of Fisheries and Oceans (DFO) continues its 204-year history of providing transport and supplies to the island. Environment Canada will manage the island's weather station, which has provided meteorological information, without interruption, since 1871.

The Sable Island horses continue to roam free, protected from any interference by humans.

Sable Island Superintendents

1801–1809	James Morris
1809–1830	Edward Hodgeson
1830–1848	Joseph Darby
1848–1855	Mathew D. McKenna
1855–1873	Philip Sherwood Dodd
1873–1884	Duncan McDonald
1884	J. H. Garroway (assistant superintendent for seven months)
1884–1912	R. J. Boutilier
1912–1919	Captain V. W. Blakeney
1919–1930	Jack Campbell
1930–1938	Charles David Faulkner
1939–1942	Don Johnson
1942–1945	Charles David Faulkner
1945–1948	Don Johnson
1948–1952	Captain Patrick Solowon
1952–1956	Charles D. Faulkner
1956–1960	Arthur Dooks

Further Reading

Armstrong, Bruce. *Sable Island, Nova Scotia's Mysterious Island of Sand.* Halifax: Formac, 1987.

Campbell, Lyall. *Sable Island, Fatal and Fertile Crescent.* Windsor: Lancelot Press, 1974.

————. *Sable Island Shipwrecks: Disaster and Survival in the North Atlantic Graveyard.* Halifax: Nimbus, 1994.

Carnochan, Janet. *Shipwrecked on Sable Island.* 1879. Edited by John L. Field, Niagara Historical Society, Pamphlet #44, 1986.

Christie, Barbara. *The Horses of Sable Island.* Porter's Lake: Pottersfield Press, 1995.

De Villiers, Marc and Sheila Hirtle. *A Dune Adrift: The Strange Origins and Curious History of Sable Island.* Toronto: McClelland & Stewart, 2004.

Farquahar, James. *Farquahar's Luck.* Halifax: Petheric Press, 1980.

Gilpin, J. Bernard. *Sable Island: Its Past History, Present Appearance, Natural History.* Halifax: Wesleyan Conference Steam Press, 1858.

Hadley, Michael. *U-Boats against Canada: German Submarines in Canadian Waters.* Kingston: McGill-Queen's University Press, 1985.

Howe, Joseph. *The Speeches and Public Lectures of the Honourable Joseph Howe, 1804–1873.* Halifax: Government of Nova Scotia, 1873.

Keough, Pat and Rosemarie Keough. *Wild and Beautiful Sable Island.* Fulford Harbour: Nahanni Productions, 1993.

Lucas, Zoe. *Wild Horses of Sable Island.* Toronto: Greey de Pencier Books, 1989.

Mitcham, Allison. *Island Keepers.* Hantsport: Lancelot Press, 1989.

Morris, James Rainstorpe. *Sable Island Journals 1801–1804.* Transcribed by Rosalee Stilwell. Halifax: Sable Island Preservation Trust, 2001.

Patterson, Rev. George. *Sable Island, Its History and Phenomena.* Halifax: Knight & Co., 1894.

Raddall, Thomas. *The Nymph and the Lamp*. Halifax: Nimbus, 1994.

———. *In My Time, A Memoir*. Toronto: McClelland & Stewart, 1976.

Richardson, Evelyn. *We Keep a Light*. Toronto: Ryerson Press, 1945.

Small, Connie. *The Lighthouse Keeper's Wife*. Orono: University of Maine Press, 1986.

To learn more about Sable Island:
The Sable Island Green Horse Society
www.greenhorsesociety.com

The Sable Island Preservation Trust
www.sabletrust.ns.ca

Photo Credits

Cover: Zoe Lucas. DFO – Coast Guard: page 96; Maritime Museum of the Atlantic: pages 102 (N-16038), 103 (N-16049); Zoe Lucas, Sable Island Green Horse Society: pages 23, 92, 105, 131, 134. Thomas Raddall Collection, Dalhousie University: page 113.

Acknowledgments

I would like to thank the staff and volunteers at the Provincial Archives of Nova Scotia, and the Harriet Irving Library, University of New Brunswick. I offer heartfelt gratitude to: Lynn-Marie Richard, assistant curator/registrar, Maritime Museum of the Atlantic, Halifax, Nova Scotia; Gisele Leblanc and April Hennigar of the Sable Island Preservation Trust, Halifax, Nova Scotia; Gerry Forbes, Environment Canada, Sable Island Station; Clark Bernat, managing director, Niagara Historical Society and Museum, Niagara, Ontario; and Gerald Faulkner and Audrey Dooks, for so patiently answering my numerous questions and requests for sources. Whenever my research uncovered discrepancies in information, I relied on first-hand writings as the definitive choice.

I am deeply indebted to those who agreed to read specific chapters so as to identify my mistakes, before I embarrassed myself in print: Chris Charland, pilot/associate air force historian/author, Directorate of Air Force Heritage and History, 1 Canadian Air Division, 22 Wing, North Bay, Ontario; Ralph Getson, curator of education, Fisheries Museum of the Atlantic, Lunenburg, Nova Scotia; Zoe Lucas, Sable Island Green Horse Society, Nova Scotia; Barry MacDonald, president, Nova Scotia Lighthouse Preservation Society; and Joan Waldron, Sable Island Preservation Trust, Halifax, Nova Scotia.

I offer a personal note of thanks to Joyce Glasner, acquisitions editor of Altitude Publishing, who shares my fascination with Sable Island, and to my editor, Jill Foran, whose suggestions and questions improved the manuscript. And, as always, thanks to my husband, Bruce Pendrel, who supports me in everything that I do.

About the Author

Johanna Bertin lives in Smithfield, New Brunswick. She has been entranced with Sable Island since she was a young girl, and researching this book was a labour of love that served only to increase her fascination with the island, and the people and horses that call it home.

She is the author of two other books: *Strange Events: Incredible Canadian Monsters, Curses, Ghosts and Other Tales*, and *Strange Events and More: Canadian Giants, Witches, Wizards, and Other Tales*, both through Altitude Publishing. She is presently researching her fourth book — *Strange Events of the East Coast*.